SHADOWS IN THE CLOUD

Navigating Threats Beyond the Surface Web

Enyinaya Okafor

Shadows in the Cloud: Navigating Threats Beyond the Surface Web

Published In Nigeria by:

Emphaloz Publishing House

www.emphaloz.com

TABLE OF CONTENTS

PREFACE

The journey to write Shadows in the Cloud began long before the first words appeared on the page. It arose from years spent standing at the crossroads of technology, vulnerability, and human consequence. As a cybersecurity expert, I've had the privilege (and sometimes the burden) of witnessing both attackers' extraordinary ingenuity and defenders' remarkable resilience. The technical battles themselves are fascinating: lines of code used as weapons, firewalls and encryption deployed as shields, and a never-ending dance of adaptation as one side innovates and the other responds. However, what struck me most deeply was not the sheer sophistication of the tools or strategies, but the very real human stories that lay beneath the surface of those digital conflicts.

Behind every breach, intrusion, or exploit is a story that cannot be summarized in headlines or statistics. It could be a small business owner witnessing years of hard work vanish overnight due to a ransomware attack. It could be a family's personal memories, which were previously trusted to the cloud, are stolen or destroyed. On a larger scale, it can refer to a community disrupted by the failure of critical infrastructure or a country dealing with the political and economic consequences of state-sponsored cyber operations. Each incident serves as a reminder that cyberspace is a human space, where choices, risks, and values intersect in ways that have a tangible impact on people's lives, just like any other physical event.

This book was not created solely to document technical exploits or recount famous breaches. It was written as a call to dig deeper and recognize the human aspects of our increasingly digital existence. The hidden web is more than just a network of machines; it also reflects the societies that create and use them. Every vulnerability reveals something about trust and accountability. Every defense represents resilience, creativity, and hope. Every attack forces us to face uncomfortable truths about power, responsibility, and our common future.

Shadows in the Cloud is therefore more than just a technical account. It is an invitation to consciousness, a prompt for thought, and a guide to action. By delving into these hidden stories, I hope to not only illuminate the stakes of cybersecurity but also to inspire readers, whether experts, leaders, or everyday digital citizens, to recognize that they, too, can play a role in shaping a safer and more equitable digital world.

FOREWORD

The world has arrived at a digital crossroads. Every day, we create networks that connect billions of people, accelerating commerce, communication, and creativity on a scale unprecedented in human history. However, the same networks that connect us also provide opportunities for exploitation, surveillance, and control. The tools we celebrate for their potential can be used to harm others. This paradox defines our era: the same infrastructure that allows for collaboration and innovation also exposes vulnerabilities that spread across individuals, organizations, and entire countries.

Shadows in the Cloud is a timely investigation into this tension. Written from a lived experience in the trenches of cybersecurity rather than a distant view of theory, it provides a perspective shaped by both study and practice. Enyinnaya Okafor has spent years navigating the hidden terrain of digital defense, witnessing attackers' ingenuity and defenders' tenacity. His voice carries the weight of those encounters, weaving together history, technology, and ethics to create a story that is both insightful and urgent.

This work is particularly powerful because it refuses to treat cybersecurity as a technical subject. Firewalls, algorithms, and protocols are important components of the story, but they do not tell the entire story. At its core, cyberspace is a human domain. Behind every breach is a family, a business, or a community of people whose lives are changed in ways that statistics cannot capture. The internet is neither safe nor dangerous; rather, it serves as a mirror for us, reflecting our choices, values, and vulnerabilities.

This book isn't just an analysis. It is a compass that guides us toward a better understanding of the digital world we live in. It does not ignore the threats to our networks, but it does emphasize the opportunities for resilience, cooperation, and ethical responsibility. In an age when fear frequently dominates technology discussions, Shadows in the Cloud provides both caution and hope. As you turn these pages, you will be invited to look beyond the surface of firewalls and breaches to discover the human stories that give them meaning. This is more than just a book about technology; it's a guide to navigating the unseen layers of cyberspace, reminding us that the future is unpredictable. It remains our shape.

INTRODUCTION

The internet has long been celebrated as a boundless frontier of knowledge, communication, and commerce. With a simple search, we can summon libraries of information, connect with people across continents, and conduct business in ways that seemed unthinkable just a generation ago. Yet, behind the glowing screens and seamless apps lies a different world, a hidden dimension of the web that thrives in obscurity. It is here, in the unseen layers of cyberspace, that shadows move quietly, shaping a parallel reality of risk, power, and secrecy.

This book, *Shadows in the Cloud: Navigating Threats Beyond the Surface Web*, explores the intricate maze of that hidden world. While the surface web, what most people use daily represents only a fraction of the internet, beneath it lie the vast depths of the Deep Web and the darker enclaves of the dark web. Within these layers exist not just forums and encrypted marketplaces, but entire communities, economies, and power structures operating beyond conventional oversight. These are the places where anonymity is currency and where both innovation and criminality intertwine.

But this exploration is not meant to sensationalize or inspire fear. Instead, it is a sober journey into understanding the realities of the hidden web and the threats that extend beyond the everyday digital experience. Cybercrime, espionage, disinformation campaigns, and clandestine trade all find their footing in these shadows, but so do stories of resistance, freedom of speech, and survival in repressive regimes. The duality of these spaces, the balance between empowerment and danger, forms the central narrative of this work.

As readers, you will be guided through the history, psychology, and technology that underpin the hidden web. From the birth of anonymous networks to the evolution of cryptocurrencies, from the rise of cyber mercenaries to the new frontiers of artificial intelligence in the shadows, this book aims to provide clarity without losing sight of complexity. Each chapter will uncover not just the threats but also the strategies individuals, organizations, and nations can use to navigate this terrain more safely.

The shadows of the cloud are not to be ignored. Whether you are a professional in cybersecurity, a student of digital culture, or simply a curious reader, understanding what lies beyond the surface web is no longer optional; it is essential. Only by acknowledging these hidden spaces and the forces that shape them can we prepare for a future where the boundaries between visible and invisible, safe and dangerous, legitimate and illicit grow ever more blurred.

CHAPTER ONE

The Unseen Layers of the Internet

The internet, as most of us know it, begins with a search bar. We type a query, press enter, and are presented with thousands, sometimes millions, of results. From recipes and travel tips to academic papers and global news outlets, the web feels infinite and endless repository of knowledge ready to serve our needs. Yet, despite its vastness, the surface web which is indexed by search engines such as Google, Bing, and Yahoo, accounts for only a small fraction of the internet's total content. The majority of what exists online resides in layers hidden from traditional access points. To understand the nature of the threats and opportunities that exist beyond the visible web, one must first grasp the boundaries of the surface.

The surface web is often described as the "tip of the iceberg." Like the portion of ice visible above the waterline, it is only a small manifestation of a much larger structure. Every website we can easily access news sites, e-commerce platforms, blogs, social media profiles, and streaming services belongs to this layer. The content here is discoverable through indexing, meaning that search engines catalog and display it to users. This is the internet of convenience: a digital marketplace, library, and town square all rolled into one. It is the layer of the web that has been monetized, regulated (to some extent), and shaped to be user-friendly.

Yet, its accessibility is also its limitation. Because the surface web is open, it is inherently a curated experience. Content is designed for public visibility, structured for search optimization, and bound by corporate policies, legal frameworks, and, in some cases, censorship. Sensitive data, academic databases behind paywalls, government records not meant for casual browsing, personal medical information, private communication logs, or corporate intranets do not reside here. They exist deeper down, shielded from indexing and invisible to traditional search. What we see on the surface is therefore a carefully controlled slice of the whole. To understand the internet in its totality, one must be willing to go beneath.

This realization that the web has hidden dimensions has long fascinated researchers, journalists, and the curious. It is the starting point of many journeys into the unseen, journeys that reveal not only technical complexity but also profound questions about privacy, power, and control. Before we confront the dangers lurking in the dark corners, it is essential to map out these unseen layers and the dynamics that govern them.

Peering into the Deep Web

Beneath the surface web lies what is commonly known as the Deep Web. Unlike the Dark Web, which has become synonymous with secrecy and criminality, the Deep Web is largely benign. It refers to all content that is not indexed by search engines. This includes academic databases, legal archives, online banking portals, medical records, and private communication tools. In many ways, the Deep Web is the infrastructure that sustains much of our daily digital lives, even if we are not always aware of it.

Imagine, for instance, a university student conducting research. When they log into their institution's online library to access journal articles, they are entering the Deep Web. These resources are not available to the general public and cannot be retrieved with a simple Google search. Similarly, when a person checks their online banking records, they are navigating a secure, unindexed part of the web designed to protect sensitive information. Corporate intranets, government systems, and subscription-based platforms all reside in this layer. Without the Deep Web, the efficiency and security of modern digital society would collapse.

Yet, the very characteristics that make the Deep Web essential, its hidden nature, its lack of indexing, and its emphasis on access controls also create fertile ground for secrecy. While most of the Deep Web is legitimate and often boring in its routine functionality, it blurs into the Dark Web at its edges. Here, anonymity becomes not just a feature but a shield. And once anonymity takes precedence over visibility, new dynamics emerge, ones that challenge the boundaries of law, ethics, and safety.

The distinction between the Deep and Dark Web is therefore critical. The Deep Web is not inherently dangerous; it is simply inaccessible to the casual browser. But for those who deliberately seek to bypass traditional pathways, specialized tools and networks can open doors to darker, less predictable domains. To peer into the Deep Web is to glimpse the scaffolding of our digital age. To go further is to risk stepping into a space where the rules shift dramatically.

The Shadowed Realm of the Dark Web

If the Deep Web represents the hidden infrastructure of modern life, the Dark Web is its most secretive chamber. Accessible only through specialized software such as Tor (The Onion Router), I2P, or Freenet, the Dark Web is intentionally concealed. Unlike the Deep Web, which is hidden because of technical or access-related reasons, the Dark Web is hidden by design. Its architecture is built to anonymize users and obscure the location of websites, creating an ecosystem where invisibility is not a side effect but the central principle.

The origins of the Dark Web are not as sinister as popular imagination suggests. Tor, for instance, was developed with funding from the United States Naval Research Laboratory to protect intelligence communications. The same qualities that allow dissidents in authoritarian regimes to communicate secure resistance to censorship, strong encryption, and the ability to obscure identities also make the Dark Web attractive to those with less noble intentions. This duality is at the heart of its complexity: the Dark Web is simultaneously a tool for freedom and a marketplace for crime.

Inside the Dark Web, one finds a mixture of communities and marketplaces. On one hand, it hosts forums where activists share information without fear of persecution, journalists exchange sensitive data with whistleblowers, and citizens of repressive nations bypass censorship. On the other, it is infamous for black markets offering illegal drugs, weapons, stolen data, counterfeit documents, and hacking services. Cryptocurrencies, particularly Bitcoin and privacy-focused alternatives such as Monero, fuel these transactions, creating a financial layer of secrecy to match the technological one.

But beyond the commerce lies something deeper: culture. The Dark Web is not merely a collection of hidden websites it is a social organism. It is sustained by communities that thrive on secrecy, trust, and reputation, paradoxical as that may seem. In an environment where identities are obscured, credibility becomes a valuable currency. Vendors build reputations through reliable transactions, forums cultivate insider knowledge, and groups form around shared interests ranging from political activism to cybercrime. The ecosystem is fragile, volatile, and constantly shifting, but it reveals something profound about human behavior given the means to act without consequence, some choose liberation, others choose exploitation.

The threats emerging from the Dark Web are not confined to its borders. Stolen data finds its way into mainstream systems, ransomware gangs recruit through its forums, and disinformation campaigns are coordinated from its channels. At the same time, its role as a sanctuary for free expression cannot be ignored. In places where governments monitor every online interaction, the Dark Web provides a rare space of autonomy. This paradox where empowerment and exploitation coexist makes the Dark Web one of the most fascinating and troubling aspects of the modern digital landscape.

Bridging the Layers: A Concluding Reflection

The unseen layers of the internet remind us that what we encounter daily is only a curated surface. Beneath lies a complex architecture of hidden systems, from the practical and essential Deep Web to the shadowed and morally ambiguous Dark Web. These layers are not separate universes; they interact with and influence the surface, shaping the digital experiences of billions of people worldwide. Understanding these dimensions is the first step toward navigating the threats they contain. Without such awareness, individuals and societies are left vulnerable to forces they cannot see but that nonetheless shape their lives.

In the chapters that follow, this book will move deeper into those shadows. We will examine how curiosity and risk-taking lead individuals into hidden networks, how criminal economies thrive in digital obscurity, how state actors weaponize anonymity, and how the illusion of privacy crumbles under the pressure of surveillance. By the end, the reader will not only understand the architecture of the hidden web but also the human stories that animate the ambitions, fears, and power struggles that unfold in the unseen corridors of the cloud.

CHAPTER TWO

From Curiosity to Chaos

The story of hidden networks is as much a tale of human ambition as it is of technological innovation. At the dawn of the internet, few imagined the scope it would one day achieve. Early networks were small, experimental, and largely academic, built to exchange information efficiently among researchers and government institutions. Security, privacy, and anonymity were afterthoughts; the internet was never intended to become the world's digital marketplace, political arena, or criminal underworld. Yet, as the web expanded, so did the need for spaces where visibility could be controlled, where surveillance could be resisted, and where information could flow outside the boundaries of authority.

The seeds of hidden networks were planted in the very foundations of digital communication. The concept of packet-switched networks, developed in the 1960s by researchers like Paul Baran and Donald Davies, was designed to create resilient communication systems that could survive nuclear attacks. This decentralized approach, where data could find multiple paths to its destination, inadvertently laid the groundwork for systems that would later prioritize anonymity over centralized control. The ARPANET, launched in 1969, connected just four universities, but its underlying architecture would eventually enable communications that could evade oversight and detection.

Hidden networks were not born out of criminal intent but from the pursuit of freedom. Governments, activists, and technologists sought ways to secure communication in an increasingly connected world. One of the earliest examples of this ambition was Tor (The Onion Router), developed in the 1990s with support from the United States Naval Research Laboratory. Its purpose was straightforward yet powerful: to allow intelligence operatives to communicate anonymously without exposing their locations or activities. Tor worked by routing internet traffic through multiple volunteer-run servers, each layer encrypting and obscuring the source of the communication hence the metaphor of "onion routing." By the time a message reached its destination, its origins were effectively hidden.

The development of Tor was driven by researchers like Paul Syverson, Michael Reed, and David Goldschlag, who understood that true anonymity required more than simple encryption. They recognized that encrypted communications could be traced through traffic analysis, observing patterns of when and where data flows, even without reading its contents. Their solution was elegant: by bouncing communications through multiple intermediary nodes, each knowing only the previous and next step in the chain, no single point in the network could reveal both the source and destination of a message.

Soon, the potential applications of such technology extended far beyond the intelligence community. Journalists saw it as a lifeline for protecting whistleblowers. The revelations of Edward Snowden in 2013 would later demonstrate how crucial such tools could be, as journalists used Tor and other anonymity networks to communicate with sources who risked imprisonment or worse for exposing government surveillance programs. Dissidents in authoritarian regimes viewed it as a shield against censorship and persecution. During the Arab Spring of 2010-2012, activists in Egypt, Tunisia, and Syria used Tor to coordinate protests and share information when their governments blocked traditional communication channels.

Academics and technologists embraced it as a tool to preserve the principle of privacy in a world where surveillance was becoming increasingly normalized. The Electronic Frontier Foundation, founded in 1990 by John Perry Barlow, Mitch Kapor, and John Gilmore, championed the development of anonymity tools as essential for preserving digital civil liberties. They argued that privacy was not about hiding wrongdoing but about preserving the space for dissent, creativity, and personal autonomy that democratic societies require.

Hidden networks promised autonomy in a digital age increasingly defined by exposure. But this promise carried with it unintended consequences. Just as anonymity could protect dissidents, it could also shield criminals. Just as censorship-resistant systems could amplify the voices of the oppressed, they could also empower markets in drugs, weapons, and stolen data. The birth of hidden networks was not a simple act of creation; it was the opening of a Pandora's box. With every advancement in encryption, obfuscation, and decentralization, new doors were opened not only for freedom but also for exploitation.

The Technical Evolution

The technological sophistication of hidden networks evolved rapidly through the 2000s. Early anonymous systems were often clunky and required significant technical knowledge to be used effectively. The original Tor browser was far from user-friendly, demanding command-line operations and manual configuration that deterred casual users. However, as the technology matured, barriers to entry plummeted.

The introduction of the Tor Browser Bundle in 2008 marked a turning point. This package simplified the process of accessing hidden networks to a single download and installation, no different from installing any other browser. Suddenly, the technical barrier that had once protected these networks from casual exploration vanished. Anyone with basic computer skills could access the Dark Web in minutes.

Parallel developments in cryptocurrency further lowered barriers to participation in hidden economies. Bitcoin, launched in 2009 by the pseudonymous Satoshi Nakamoto, provided a payment system that appeared to offer the same anonymity as the networks themselves. While Bitcoin transactions are actually pseudonymous rather than anonymous recorded on a public ledger but tied to wallet addresses rather than real names the perception of anonymity was sufficient to fuel the growth of underground markets.

The combination of accessible anonymity tools and perceived anonymous payments created a perfect storm. The transition from idealism to pragmatism was swift. By the early 2000s, online forums began experimenting with these technologies, creating spaces where users could communicate without fear of reprisal. Soon after, marketplaces emerged, modeled after e-commerce platforms on the surface web but driven by the promise of anonymity. These were not the mainstream spaces of Amazon or eBay but underground bazaars where illegal drugs, counterfeit goods, and hacking services could be purchased with cryptocurrencies.

The Silk Road, launched in 2011 by Ross Ulbricht under the pseudonym "Dread Pirate Roberts," became the most notorious example of how hidden networks could enable criminal enterprise. The marketplace operated like a sophisticated e-commerce platform, complete with user reviews, vendor ratings, and customer service departments. However, instead of selling books or electronics, it facilitated the sale of narcotics, with transactions conducted in Bitcoin and goods shipped through conventional postal services.

Hidden networks had moved from a vision of digital liberation into a theater of clandestine commerce. The trajectory from creation to corruption is not unique to the internet.

Throughout history, innovations designed to empower humanity have often been co-opted for darker purposes. The printing press spread knowledge but also propaganda. Nuclear technology provides energy but also weapons. Similarly, hidden networks have become dual-use tools: indispensable for freedom, indispensable for crime. This duality lies at the heart of their story, and it is what makes navigating the shadows so complex.

Anonymity and Its Double Edge

The pursuit of anonymity is one of humanity's oldest impulses. Masks, codes, disguises, and secret societies have existed for centuries, offering protection, power, and mystique. From the anonymous pamphlets that fueled the American Revolution to the underground railroads that guided slaves to freedom, anonymity has long been both a shield for the vulnerable and a tool for social change. In the digital age, anonymity takes on new dimensions, fueled by encryption, decentralized systems, and networks designed to obscure identity. But anonymity is never neutral. It empowers and endangers, liberates and corrupts, shields the innocent and emboldens the guilty. It is, in essence, a double-edged sword.

For many, anonymity online is not a luxury but a necessity. Journalists rely on it to protect sources who risk their careers, freedom, or lives to expose corruption and wrongdoing. The Washington Post's reporting on government surveillance programs, The Guardian's coverage of the Panama Papers, and countless investigations into corporate malfeasance all depend on the ability to communicate anonymously with whistleblowers. Without anonymity tools, many of the most important stories of the past decade would never have come to light.

Activists use anonymity to organize in repressive environments where political dissent can result in imprisonment, torture, or death. In Hong Kong during the 2019 pro-democracy protests, demonstrators used mesh networking apps and Tor to coordinate activities when the government threatened to monitor conventional communication channels. Iranian dissidents have long relied on anonymity tools to circumvent government censorship and surveillance. For LGBTQ+ individuals in countries where their identities are criminalized, anonymous networks provide vital spaces for community and support.

Everyday users depend on anonymity for privacy in a world where corporations track their all clicks, and government agencies monitor digital activity at unprecedented scales. The rise of surveillance capitalism, where personal data becomes the raw material for targeted advertising and behavioral manipulation, has made privacy tools essential for anyone seeking to maintain autonomy over their digital lives. Tor usage spikes during political crises, suggesting that even in democratic societies, citizens recognize the value of anonymous communication when tensions rise.

Yet, the same qualities that safeguard freedom also provide cover for exploitation. Criminal organizations thrive in anonymous ecosystems, where identities can be fabricated, reputations manipulated, and transactions concealed. The structure of anonymity networks makes them ideal for criminal enterprise: transactions can be conducted without revealing personal information, communications can be encrypted end-to-end, and the decentralized nature of these systems makes them resistant to takedown efforts.

Darknet markets, fueled by cryptocurrencies, rely on anonymity as their foundation. Without it, the trade in narcotics, weapons, human trafficking, and stolen data would collapse. These markets operate with sophisticated feedback systems, escrow services, and customer support all the trappings of legitimate e-commerce, but applied to illegal goods and services. The largest markets process millions of dollars in transactions monthly, creating entire economies that exist parallel to the legitimate world.

Anonymity makes possible the creation of entire underground economies, invisible to traditional oversight. These economies are not merely black markets but complex systems with their own norms, governance structures, and cultural practices. Vendors develop reputations that can be worth thousands of dollars in future business. Forums emerge to discuss best practices for everything from operational security to customer service. In many ways, these hidden economies mirror legitimate markets, but with the crucial difference that they operate entirely outside the reach of traditional law enforcement.

The Psychology of Hidden Communities

The consequences extend beyond commerce. Cyberattacks, ransomware campaigns, and espionage operations all exploit anonymity. Hackers conceal their identities while infiltrating systems, holding corporations and governments hostage with encrypted demands for payment. The 2017 WannaCry ransomware attack affected over 300,000 computers in 150 countries, causing billions in damages. The perpetrators demanded payment in Bitcoin to anonymous wallet addresses, using the same anonymity tools that protect dissidents to shield themselves from prosecution.

State actors use hidden networks to conduct espionage, disguise propaganda campaigns, and destabilize adversaries. Russian intelligence services have used Tor and other anonymity tools to mask the origins of disinformation campaigns, while North Korean hackers have used these networks to conduct devastating attacks on financial institutions and critical infrastructure. In these contexts, anonymity is not merely a shield but a weapon, enabling aggression without accountability.

At the same time, the illusion of anonymity can be dangerous. Many who venture into hidden networks believe themselves invincible, shielded from detection. History tells a different story. High-profile arrests of darknet market administrators, hackers, and criminals reveal that anonymity, while powerful, is never absolute. The arrest of Ross Ulbricht in 2013, the takedown of AlphaBay and Hansa markets in 2017, and countless other law enforcement operations demonstrate that determined investigators can pierce the veil of anonymity through a combination of technical analysis, operational security failures, and human error.

Metadata, operational mistakes, and law enforcement infiltration have repeatedly pierced the veil. Users who believe they are anonymous often leave digital breadcrumbs through their browsing habits, writing styles, or operational patterns. The use of the same username across multiple platforms, correlations in online activity patterns, and mistakes in operational security have led to numerous arrests. The story of anonymity is therefore not only about empowerment but also about vulnerability. Those who misuse it often underestimate the patience and persistence of those who pursue them.

What makes anonymity especially fascinating is the culture it creates. In hidden networks, trust becomes paradoxically vital. Users who cannot reveal their real identities must establish reputations through other means: reliability, consistency, and peer validation. This creates unique social dynamics where pseudonymous identities can become more trusted than many real-world personas.

Vendors in darknet markets build credibility by fulfilling orders faithfully, providing quality products, and maintaining consistent communication with customers. A vendor with hundreds of positive reviews can command premium prices and customer loyalty, despite never revealing their real identity. Forum participants earn respect by sharing valuable information, providing technical support, or contributing to community discussions. Moderators and administrators of hidden services often wield significant influence despite being known only by their pseudonyms.

In these environments, anonymity does not eliminate accountability, it reshapes it. A pseudonym, if trusted, can carry as much weight as a real name. Some pseudonymous identities in hidden networks become legendary figures, known and respected by thousands of users who would never recognize them in the physical world. This creates a unique form of reputation economy where trust is built through actions rather than credentials, consistency rather than credentials.

How Curiosity Breeds Risk

Curiosity is one of humanity's most defining traits. It drives exploration, innovation, and discovery, pushing us beyond the boundaries of the known. From ancient explorers who sailed beyond the horizon to modern scientists who probe the depths of space, curiosity has been the engine of human progress. Yet, it is also a source of risk. Just as children might touch fire to learn its heat, so too do individuals venture into the hidden web to see what lies beyond the surface. Curiosity opens doors, but it also blinds us to danger. In the world of hidden networks, curiosity can be both a teacher and a trap.

For many, the journey into the Dark Web begins innocently. A story in the news about cybercrime piques interest. A documentary about digital privacy sparks intrigue. A conversation about censorship resistance inspires exploration.

The media coverage of major darknet market takedowns often has the unintended consequence of advertising these networks to curious individuals who had never heard of them before.

With free tools like the Tor browser just a download away, the barrier to entry is low. The installation process is no more complex than downloading any other software, and numerous tutorials and guides make the process accessible to users with minimal technical knowledge. The first steps are often tentative, browsing forums, exploring directories, or testing out anonymous communication. Many users begin with entirely legal activities: reading censored news, exploring privacy tools, or simply satisfying curiosity about what lies beyond the surface web.

Yet, these small acts can lead to a slippery slope, where curiosity becomes entanglement. The structure of hidden networks naturally leads users from innocuous content to more extreme material. Links between sites create pathways that can gradually expose users to increasingly illicit content. Forums that begin with discussions of privacy tools often contain sections dedicated to more questionable activities. The recommendation algorithms that guide exploration on the surface web don't exist in hidden networks, but social recommendations and curious exploration can lead users down similar rabbit holes.

The risks of such exploration are manifold. Technically, hidden networks are rife with vulnerabilities. Many sites are operated by individuals with limited security expertise, making them prone to compromise. Malicious websites can infect devices with malware, compromising not only the user's anonymity but also their personal data. These malware infections can be particularly dangerous because they may be designed to de-anonymize users, tracking their real IP addresses and activities even when they believe they are protected.

Law enforcement agencies actively monitor certain hubs, turning curiosity into evidence. The FBI and other agencies operate honeypots, fake marketplaces and forums designed to attract and identify users. Simply visiting certain sites can result in an individual's IP address being logged, even if they never engage in any illegal activity. The legal implications of even browsing certain types of content can be severe, with possession of certain materials being criminalized regardless of intent.

Psychological risks are equally potent. Exposure to disturbing content, whether images of violence, extremist propaganda, or exploitative materials, can leave lasting impressions. The hidden web contains some of the most disturbing content available online, from graphic violence to exploitation of children. Many users who venture into these networks out of curiosity find themselves exposed to content they were not prepared to encounter.

What begins as curiosity can quickly spiral into trauma or desensitization. The normalization of extreme content that occurs in some hidden communities can gradually shift users' perceptions of what is acceptable. Regular exposure to illegal marketplaces, for example, can make such activities seem routine rather than criminal. This psychological impact can persist long after users stop accessing hidden networks.

There is also the risk of temptation. Hidden networks often dangle forbidden fruits: cheap drugs, counterfeit goods, stolen credit cards, or illicit services. For some, the allure is irresistible. What begins as exploration turns into participation. A purchase made "just to see if it works" becomes a gateway to deeper involvement. The ease of access and apparent anonymity can lower the psychological barriers to illegal activity.

The gamification aspects of some hidden communities can also drive deeper involvement. Forums with reputation systems, achievement badges, and social status based on contributions can create addictive dynamics. Users may find themselves spending increasing amounts of time in these communities, gradually adopting their norms and values. In this way, curiosity becomes not only a risk but a catalyst, transforming passive exploration into active engagement. The line between observer and participant blurs.

The Constructive Power of Informed Curiosity

But curiosity is not inherently dangerous. It can also be the seed of awareness. Journalists and researchers who venture into hidden networks often do so out of curiosity, seeking to understand their dynamics. Their work brings visibility to spaces that thrive on secrecy, providing insights that help societies respond to threats. Investigative journalists like Brian Krebs, who have spent years documenting cybercrime operations, rely on careful exploration of hidden networks to understand and expose criminal enterprises.

Academic researchers studying online communities, digital economies, and cybersecurity often depend on access to hidden networks to conduct their work. Studies of darknet markets have provided valuable insights into drug distribution networks, while research on extremist forums has helped identify radicalization patterns. This research, conducted with appropriate ethical oversight and security precautions, contributes to our understanding of these phenomena and informs policy responses.

Cybersecurity experts, too, rely on curiosity to probe vulnerabilities, test defenses, and anticipate future risks. Threat intelligence analysts monitor hidden networks to identify emerging threats, track criminal innovations, and understand adversary capabilities. This work requires careful navigation of dangerous spaces, but it provides essential intelligence for protecting organizations and individuals from cyber threats.

In these cases, curiosity becomes a tool for protection rather than peril. The difference lies in preparation, purpose, and precaution. Professional researchers and investigators approach hidden networks with specific objectives, appropriate security measures, and institutional support. They understand the risks they face and have protocols for managing them.

The challenge, then, lies in managing curiosity. Like any form of exploration, it requires preparation, caution, and guidance. Mountain climbers don't attempt Everest without training and equipment; similarly, exploration of hidden networks requires digital literacy, security awareness, and psychological preparation. Without these, curiosity becomes reckless, leading individuals into situations they cannot control. With them, it becomes informed exploration, a way to illuminate shadows without being consumed by them.

Educational approaches to digital literacy increasingly recognize the importance of preparing individuals for the realities of the internet, including its hidden corners. Teaching users about the risks and realities of online anonymity, the existence of hidden networks, and the importance of digital security can help them make informed decisions about their online activities.

The difference is subtle but vital, marking the boundary between discovery and disaster. Informed curiosity guided by knowledge, constrained by ethics, and protected by security measures can contribute to understanding and awareness. Uninformed curiosity driven by impulse, unprotected by precautions, and unguided by purpose often leads to harmful consequences.

Curiosity will always drive people into the unknown. It is what has propelled humanity across oceans, into space, and now into the digital depths. The same impulse that led early internet users to explore bulletin board systems and the early web now draws individuals into hidden networks. This exploration is natural and, in many ways, healthy represents the human desire to understand and experience the full scope of our digital world.

But in the shadows of the cloud, curiosity comes with a price. To navigate hidden networks is to walk a fine line between knowledge and risk, between empowerment and entanglement. Those who fail to recognize this balance often find that curiosity does not merely open doors, it can also close them, trapping the unwary in chaos. The stories of individuals whose lives have been disrupted by their forays into hidden networks serve as cautionary tales about the importance of approaching these spaces with appropriate preparation and caution.

The journey from curiosity to chaos encapsulates the paradox of hidden networks. Born out of noble ambitions, these systems offer both sanctuary and peril. Anonymity, their defining feature, protects and empowers even as it enables exploitation. The same tools that allow dissidents to organize against oppression enable criminals to organize against society. The same networks that provide safe harbor for whistleblowers provide a marketplace for illegal goods and services.

Curiosity, the human impulse that draws individuals into the shadows, offers pathways to discovery but also to danger. The democratization of access to hidden networks means that the same tools available to professional researchers and activists are also available to anyone with an internet connection and a few minutes to spare. This democratization brings both opportunities and risks.

Together, these forces shape the landscape of the unseen internet, a place where freedom and threat, empowerment and vulnerability coexist in uneasy tension. The challenge for individuals, communities, and societies is learning to navigate this landscape responsibly, maximizing the benefits while minimizing the risks.

The story is far from simple. Hidden networks are not merely havens for criminals nor utopias for dissidents. They are complex ecosystems, shaped by technology, psychology, and culture. They reflect the best and worst of human nature, amplified by the power of anonymity and the allure of secrecy. To navigate them requires more than technical skill; it requires wisdom, caution, and an understanding of the forces that drive people from curiosity into chaos.

The evolution of hidden networks continues, driven by ongoing tensions between privacy and security, freedom and control, and curiosity and caution. As these networks become more sophisticated and accessible, the importance of understanding their dynamics becomes ever greater. The choices we make about how to engage with these systems individually and collectively will shape not only their development but also their impact on society.

In the next chapter, we will move deeper into this terrain, examining the rise of cybercrime in the clouded corners of the web. Here, the dynamics of anonymity and curiosity give way to organized markets, digital mercenaries, and economies built entirely in the shadows. It is there that the full consequences of hidden networks become clear, not as abstract risks but as tangible threats shaping the security and stability of the world we inhabit.

CHAPTER THREE

Cybercrime in the Clouded Corners

The story of cybercrime in hidden networks is inseparable from the rise of illicit marketplaces. These marketplaces, often referred to as darknet markets, mirror the design of legitimate e-commerce platforms but operate with a radical difference: they exist entirely in the shadows. They do not rely on traditional payment systems, do not subject themselves to regulatory oversight, and do not demand verified identities from their users. Instead, they thrive on anonymity, cryptocurrencies, and a culture of secrecy that sustains their growth.

One of the most notorious examples was the Silk Road, a darknet market launched in 2011. Modeled after mainstream e-commerce giants, it offered thousands of listings, primarily illegal drugs, accessible only through the Tor network and payable exclusively in Bitcoin. What set Silk Road apart was not merely its scale but its philosophy. Its founder, Ross Ulbricht, operating under the pseudonym "Dread Pirate Roberts" framed it as a libertarian experiment, a digital free market beyond government control. For a time, it succeeded, becoming the blueprint for countless successors.

When Silk Road was dismantled by the FBI in 2013, it was not the end but the beginning of an era. Within weeks, new marketplaces emerged, often larger and more sophisticated than their predecessors. Platforms such as AlphaBay, Hansa, and Dream Market expanded the range of goods and services on offer: counterfeit documents, stolen credit card numbers, hacking tools, weapons, and even alleged assassination services. These platforms introduced innovations such as escrow systems, customer reviews, and vendor ratings, mimicking the trust-building mechanisms of legitimate online commerce. To many observers, the ingenuity was unsettling. Here were platforms designed with the same user experience principles as Amazon but dedicated to enabling crime.

The resilience of these marketplaces lies in their adaptability. Law enforcement takedowns create temporary disruptions, but replacements quickly appear. Some operate for years, amassing millions in revenue before collapsing; others vanish overnight, sometimes in "exit scams" where administrators steal user funds. The cycle is relentless, reflecting both the demand for illicit trade and the ease with which hidden networks can host it.

What is striking about these marketplaces is not only the volume of trade but also the normalization of criminal activity. Buyers leave reviews of drug quality, vendors compete for customer loyalty, and forums discuss best practices for secure transactions. In this way, the hidden web cultivates a parallel economy that mirrors the surface web in structure but diverges radically in purpose. It transforms crime into commerce, danger into routine, and illegality into business as usual.

Weapons, Data, and Digital Smuggling

While drugs remain the most prominent commodity in darknet markets, they are far from the only one. Hidden networks have created a space where almost anything can be commodified, provided there is demand and a buyer willing to pay in cryptocurrency. Among the most troubling categories are weapons, stolen data, and services designed to undermine security systems.

The sale of weapons online is particularly alarming. Firearms, explosives, and modifications are often advertised on darknet platforms. Though many listings are scams either traps set by law enforcement or opportunistic fraudsters, the mere presence of such markets creates opportunities for trafficking. For those who succeed in purchasing, the consequences extend far beyond the digital realm, feeding into real-world violence and instability. The accessibility of weapons through hidden networks undermines national regulations and international efforts to control arms trafficking, shifting power into the hands of those who can navigate these darkened corners.

Even more pervasive is the trade in stolen data. In a world where data is often described as the "new oil," breaches of corporate, governmental, and personal systems produce a steady supply of valuable commodities. Credit card numbers, bank account credentials, medical records, and entire identity profiles are sold in bulk, fueling fraud and identity theft on a massive scale. Data breaches that make headlines often represent only the visible tip; the real story unfolds in hidden markets, where compromised information is bought and sold quietly, without public awareness. For corporations, the financial costs are staggering. For individuals, the damage can be personal and enduring, with identities hijacked and lives being disrupted.

Closely linked to data markets is the trade in hacking tools and services. “Ransomware-as-a-service” packages, distributed through hidden forums, allow even those with minimal technical skill to launch devastating attacks. Botnets can be rented, phishing kits purchased, and malware customized to specific targets. This commodification of cybercrime lowers the barrier to entry, enabling a new generation of criminals to operate with professional tools. The result is an ecosystem where cyberattacks are no longer the domain of elite hackers but are accessible to anyone willing to pay.

This phenomenon is sometimes described as digital smuggling. Just as smugglers in the physical world move contraband across borders, digital smugglers move data, tools, and illicit goods across the invisible borders of the web. The risks are lower, the costs minimal, and the rewards substantial. A smuggler no longer needs ships or secret tunnels; they need only a computer, an internet connection, and the willingness to step into the shadows. The consequences, however, ripple outward, undermining financial systems, destabilizing institutions, and eroding trust in the very fabric of the digital age.

The sheer variety of commodities available in hidden markets illustrates a sobering truth: if something has value, it will eventually find its way into the shadows. Whether weapons of war, stolen identities, or tools of deception, hidden networks transform them into tradeable assets. This is not merely crime as we once understood it; it is crime adapted to the digital environment, operating at a scale and speed unimaginable in the physical world.

The Rise of Cyber Mercenaries

Perhaps the most disturbing trend to emerge from the clouded corners of the web is the rise of cyber mercenaries. These are individuals or groups who offer hacking and cyberattack services for hire, functioning much like soldiers of fortune in the digital realm. Unlike traditional hackers motivated by ideology, curiosity, or personal gain, mercenaries are professionals, motivated primarily by profit. Their clients may range from criminals and corporations to political movements and state actors. What unites these relationships is the outsourcing of power: the ability to inflict harm or gain advantage without bearing direct responsibility.

Cyber mercenaries thrive in hidden networks for several reasons. First, anonymity provides them with protection, allowing them to advertise their services without exposing themselves. Second, cryptocurrencies offer a convenient and relatively untraceable method of payment. Third, the demand for their services is vast. Corporations may hire mercenaries to sabotage competitors. Political actors may seek their assistance in spreading disinformation or disrupting opponents. Criminals may use them to gain access to secure systems or to conduct large-scale fraud.

The range of services offered is astonishing. Distributed Denial of Service (DDoS) attacks, designed to overwhelm websites and render them inaccessible, can be purchased for a few hundred dollars. More sophisticated attacks penetrating secure databases, deploying ransomware, or creating advanced malware command higher fees but are well within the reach of determined clients. Some mercenaries even offer customer support, ensuring their clients can deploy the tools effectively. The professionalization of these services is one of the most troubling aspects of the phenomenon, signaling that cybercrime has evolved from an underground subculture into a structured industry.

The consequences of cyber mercenary activity are profound. For corporations, they represent a constant threat to intellectual property, competitive stability, and consumer trust. For governments, they pose risks to national security, critical infrastructure, and democratic processes. For individuals, they increase the likelihood of personal data theft, fraud, and exposure to cyberattacks. The invisible nature of these assaults makes them especially dangerous. Victims may not even realize they have been targeted until long after the damage is done.

Perhaps the most unsettling dimension is the blurred line between mercenaries and state actors. In some cases, governments tacitly support or even directly employ mercenaries to conduct operations that provide plausible deniability. If a cyberattack is traced back to a hidden network, attribution becomes difficult, allowing states to deny involvement while reaping the benefits of disruption. In this sense, cyber mercenaries are not merely criminals but pawns in a larger geopolitical game. Their existence complicates the already fragile landscape of international relations, where accountability is elusive and aggression can occur without warning.

The rise of cyber mercenaries is a natural extension of the hidden web's dynamics. It is the professionalization of cybercrime, the outsourcing of digital warfare, and the commodification of power in the age of shadows. What once required deep technical expertise and ideological motivation is now available as a service, purchasable in the same way one might order food delivery or transportation. The implications are staggering: a world where digital violence can be outsourced with ease, leaving victims vulnerable and perpetrators invisible.

The hidden networks of the internet are not merely obscure spaces, they are engines of crime, powered by anonymity, fueled by demand, and shaped by innovation. Marketplaces transform illegality into commerce. Weapons, data, and tools flow like contraband through invisible pipelines. Mercenaries offer their skills to the highest bidder, blurring the line between crime and war. Together, these phenomena create a digital ecosystem of unprecedented risk, one that touches individuals, corporations, and nations alike.

What makes cybercrime in the clouded corners particularly dangerous is not just its scale but its adaptability. Marketplaces adapt after takedowns. Criminals innovate to stay ahead of law enforcement. Mercenaries evolve their services to meet new demands. This is an ecosystem in constant motion, a hydra that grows new heads each time one is cut off. It is a reminder that crime, like technology itself, is dynamically shifting, always seeking new avenues for growth.

In the chapters ahead, we will move beyond the mechanics of crime to explore the human dimension of the hidden web. Who are the people drawn into these spaces? What psychological forces drive them to embrace anonymity, to trust strangers, to risk everything in pursuit of power, profit, or belonging? To understand cybercrime fully, we must look not only at the systems that enable it but at the minds and motivations of those who inhabit the shadows.

CHAPTER FOUR

The Psychology of the Hidden User

Behind every anonymous username in the hidden web lies a human being with motives that are often complex, layered, and deeply psychological. It is easy to imagine the hidden user as a faceless villain, operating in shadows with malicious intent. Yet, to reduce them to caricature is to miss the deeper truths. The psychology of hidden users cannot be understood through binary categories of "good" and "evil." Instead, their actions emerge from powerful human drivers' fear, greed, and the desire for power.

The Architecture of Fear

Fear is perhaps the most universal motivator driving individuals into the digital shadows. This fear manifests in multiple dimensions, each creating its own pathway to anonymity. Many who turn to hidden networks, doing so not to exploit others but to shield themselves from perceived or real threats. Journalists fearing surveillance find themselves alongside activists fearing persecution, whistleblowers fearing retaliation, and everyday individuals fearing the erosion of privacy all seeking the refuge of anonymity.

The fear that drives users to hidden networks is rarely simple paranoia. In authoritarian regimes, where expressing dissent can result in imprisonment or death, the hidden web becomes a lifeline for free expression. Journalists in countries with state-controlled media use encrypted channels and anonymous networks to communicate with sources and publish censored stories. For them, the shadows are not a choice but a necessity for survival and professional integrity.

Yet fear extends beyond political persecution. In democratic societies, the surveillance apparatus of both governments and corporations has created a different kind of anxiety, the fear of total transparency. Citizens concerned about data collection, behavioral tracking, and the monetization of their private lives seek anonymity not because they have something illegal to hide, but because they believe privacy itself is under assault. This defensive fear transforms ordinary people into hidden users, pushing them toward networks that promise escape from omnipresent monitoring.

The psychology of fear in hidden networks creates a feedback loop that intensifies over time. Initial anxieties about surveillance or persecution are often magnified by immersion in communities where such fears are validated and amplified. Fear begets paranoia, and paranoia drives deeper engagement with hidden systems. Users begin to see threats everywhere, interpreting benign events through the lens of persecution or surveillance. This psychological transformation can be protective maintaining operational security in genuinely dangerous environments, but it can also be destructive, creating isolation and radicalization.

What makes fear particularly potent in hidden networks is its ability to blur the line between legitimate caution and pathological paranoia. The same psychological mechanisms that protect a journalist from state retaliation can transform an ordinary citizen into someone who views all authority as inherently threatening. Fear, once awakened, becomes self-perpetuating, creating psychological dependencies on anonymity that persist long after the original threat has passed.

The Machinery of Greed

While fear drives many into the shadows seeking protection, greed transforms the hidden web into fertile ground for exploitation and crime. The psychology of greed in anonymous networks differs significantly from traditional criminal motivation. Here, the allure lies not merely in wealth but in the promise of consequence-free enrichment, money earned without oversight, taxation, or accountability.

The hidden web magnifies greed by removing traditional barriers to criminal enterprise. Physical crime requires proximity, networks, and face-to-face interaction which create vulnerabilities. Digital crime in anonymous networks, by contrast, offers scale without exposure. A single individual can operate multiple sophisticated scams, reaching thousands of victims across continents while maintaining complete anonymity. This psychological distance between perpetrator and victim reduces empathy and moral constraint, enabling levels of exploitation that would be psychologically difficult in face-to-face interactions.

Greed in hidden networks often begins with rationalization. Users convince themselves that they are merely "leveling the playing field" against corporations or governments that they perceive as exploitative. Hackers justify breaching systems as exposing security flaws. Sellers of stolen data frame their activities as redistributing wealth from the privileged to the clever. These rationalizations serve important psychological functions, allowing individuals to maintain positive self-images while engaging in harmful activities.

The economics of hidden markets create unique psychological pressures that intensify greedy behavior. Unlike traditional markets, where reputation and relationships develop over years, hidden markets are often ephemeral. Users know that markets may be shut down by law enforcement at any time, creating pressure to maximize profits quickly. This urgency generates a boom-and-bust psychology where users alternate between periods of intense activity and forced inactivity.

The anonymity that protects greedy users also isolates them. Without the social bonds that typically constrain antisocial behavior, individuals can become consumed by pure profit maximization. The lack of genuine relationships in hidden networks means that other users are viewed primarily as opportunities for exploitation rather than as human beings deserving consideration. This psychological dehumanization is essential to understanding how ordinary individuals can engage in extraordinarily harmful behavior within hidden systems.

The Intoxication of Power

Beyond fear and greed lies a deeper, more complex motivator: the desire for power. Power in hidden networks manifests in forms rarely available in the surface world, creating psychological experiences that can be profoundly addictive. For many hidden users, the ability to wield influence while remaining invisible represents the ultimate form of agency control without accountability, impact without consequence.

The power dynamics of hidden networks are fundamentally different from those in conventional society. In the surface world, power is typically linked to visible markers of wealth, position, credentials, and social connections. In hidden networks, these traditional sources of authority are irrelevant. Power flows instead to those who possess technical knowledge, insider information, or the ability to provide scarce services. This inversion creates opportunities for individuals who may be powerless in their offline lives to become influential figures in hidden communities.

For hackers, the pursuit of power often manifests as a need to demonstrate technical superiority. The act of breaching supposedly secure systems provides psychological satisfaction that goes far beyond any financial gain. Each successful intrusion becomes a validation of intelligence and skill, proving the hacker's ability to outwit professionals and institutions. This power is particularly intoxicating because it allows individuals to challenge authority figures, government agencies, corporations, and security experts who would be completely inaccessible in ordinary circumstances.

The administrators and moderators of hidden networks wield a different but equally compelling form of power. They control information flows, determine community norms, and decide who belongs and who is excluded. For individuals who may feel marginalized or ignored in their offline communities, the ability to shape digital environments can be profoundly empowering. They become gatekeepers of knowledge, arbiters of disputes, and architects of alternative social orders.

Power in hidden networks is also deeply connected to the ability to disrupt and destabilize existing systems. For extremists and ideologues, hidden networks provide platforms for spreading messages and coordinating activities that would be impossible in monitored environments. The power here lies not in building something new but in tearing down existing structures. This destructive power appeals particularly to individuals who feel victimized or oppressed by current systems, offering them the ability to strike back in ways that are both anonymous and potentially devastating.

The psychology of power in hidden networks creates its own pathologies. Users who become accustomed to wielding influence without accountability often struggle to function in environments where their actions have visible consequences. The intoxication of anonymous power can lead to increasingly risky behavior as users seek to maintain or expand their influence. Like other forms of addiction, the pursuit of power in hidden networks often escalates, driving individuals toward more extreme actions to achieve the same psychological satisfaction.

Communities Built on Secrecy

The psychology of hidden users cannot be fully understood in isolation; it is fundamentally shaped by the communities they form and inhabit. Unlike the surface web, where identities are often anchored in verifiable reality, hidden networks cultivate communities built entirely on constructed personas and shared secrecy. This creates a fascinating paradox: how do individuals develop trust and social bonds when all traditional markers of identity are absent or unreliable?

Hidden communities have developed sophisticated mechanisms to cultivate credibility in the absence of conventional identity markers. Reputation systems become the primary currency of trust, with users building digital personas through consistent behavior over time. These systems often involve complex webs of mutual validation users vouch for each other's reliability, creating networks of trust that can span years and multiple platforms.

The process of building trust in hidden communities requires a different kind of psychological investment than surface-world relationships. Users must judge character and reliability based solely on digital interactions, developing heightened sensitivity to subtle cues about trustworthiness. This creates communities of individuals who become experts at reading between the lines, interpreting minimal information to make critical decisions about whom to trust with money, information, or personal safety.

Vendor ratings and escrow services in hidden marketplaces represent formalized attempts to solve the trust problem, but they create their own psychological dynamics. Users must balance the desire for the best deals with the need for reliability, often developing sophisticated risk assessment skills. The constant evaluation of trust and risk creates a heightened state of awareness that shapes all interactions within hidden communities.

The Norms of Shadowlands

What emerges from these trust-building mechanisms is not chaos but a different kind of social order. Hidden communities develop their own norms, hierarchies, and codes of conduct that can be remarkably stable despite the absence of traditional authority structures. These informal systems of governance reveal important truths about human psychology and our innate drive to create social organization even in the most unlikely circumstances.

In darknet marketplaces, elaborate systems of professional conduct emerge organically. Vendors compete not only on price and product quality but also on customer service, dispute resolution, and community reputation. Many develop business practices that mirror legitimate enterprises offering guarantees, maintaining customer databases, and building brand loyalty. The absence of legal recourse makes reputation even more valuable than in conventional markets, creating powerful incentives for fair dealing.

Hidden forums develop their own cultural norms around information sharing, privacy protection, and community behavior. New members must learn unwritten rules about what information is acceptable to request, how to demonstrate value to the community, and when to remain silent. These norms are enforced through social pressure, moderation, and ultimately exclusion for those who violate community standards.

The psychology of norm formation in hidden communities reveals how humans adapt social instincts to novel environments. Even in spaces designed for anonymity and rule-breaking, users create structures of accountability and mutual obligation. This suggests that the drive to create social order is so fundamental to human psychology that it emerges even when traditional mechanisms of authority and enforcement are absent.

The Fragility of Secret Bonds

Despite their sophistication, communities built on secrecy remain inherently fragile. The same anonymity that protects users also makes them vulnerable to infiltration, deception, and betrayal. This creates a fundamental psychological tension that defines life in hidden communities: the need to trust others while maintaining constant vigilance against threats.

Law enforcement infiltration represents one of the most significant psychological pressures on hidden communities. The knowledge that any community member could be an undercover agent creates paranoia that can poison social relationships. Users must balance the benefits of community participation against the risks of exposure, leading to a culture of measured engagement where individuals carefully calibrate how much of themselves to reveal.

Internal conflicts and scams further destabilize hidden communities. When trust is broken, whether through market exit scams, doxing incidents, or interpersonal betrayals, the effects ripple through entire networks. Unlike surface-world communities, where damaged relationships can often be repaired through mediation or time, hidden communities have fewer mechanisms for rebuilding trust. The result is often community fragmentation or dissolution.

This fragility creates unique psychological pressures for hidden users. They must constantly evaluate not only whom to trust but how much to invest emotionally in relationships that could disappear at any moment. This psychological guardedness can become habitual, affecting users' ability to form genuine connections even outside hidden networks.

Escaping Reality through the Shadows

For many hidden users, the allure of anonymous networks lies not in crime or ideology but in the opportunity for complete psychological transformation. The hidden web magnifies the internet's capacity for escapism, offering not merely distraction from reality but the possibility of creating alternative identities and realities entirely unconstrained by physical limitations or social conventions.

This digital transformation serves multiple psychological functions. For individuals struggling with aspects of their offline identity, whether physical appearance, social status, gender expression, or personal history, hidden networks offer spaces where these constraints become irrelevant. Users can experiment with different personas, exploring aspects of themselves that might be suppressed or socially unacceptable in their regular lives.

The psychology of identity play in hidden networks reveals important truths about human self-concept and the role of social validation in identity formation. When freed from the constraints of consistent identity, many users discover aspects of themselves that were previously unknown or unexpressed. This can be profoundly liberating, allowing for psychological growth and self-exploration that might be impossible in conventional social settings.

However, this freedom comes with psychological risks. The ability to constantly reinvent oneself can lead to identity diffusion, where users lose touch with their core sense of self. The validation received from hidden community interactions may feel more authentic than offline relationships, creating psychological dependencies on digital personas that are ultimately unstable and artificial.

Therapeutic Escape and Its Shadow

Hidden networks often serve therapeutic functions for users dealing with trauma, mental illness, or social marginalization. Anonymous support groups provide spaces for sharing experiences that might be too stigmatized for surface-web discussion. Individuals dealing with addiction, abuse, or mental health crises can find understanding and support from others with similar experiences without fear of professional or social consequences.

This therapeutic dimension of hidden networks reveals their potential for genuine benefit. Many users report feeling more authentic and understood in anonymous communities than in their offline relationships. The ability to share difficult experiences without fear of judgment can be psychologically healing, providing emotional support that might otherwise be unavailable.

Yet the therapeutic benefits of hidden networks often come intertwined with destructive elements. Supporting communities can become enabling environments, where harmful behaviors are normalized rather than challenged. Anonymous advice may lack the accountability and professional expertise necessary for addressing serious psychological issues. Users may substitute digital support for professional treatment, potentially worsening their underlying problems.

The escapist function of hidden networks can also become pathological when it replaces rather than supplements real-world coping mechanisms. Users who rely primarily on anonymous communities for emotional support may neglect offline relationships and responsibilities, creating a cycle of isolation that reinforces their dependence on hidden networks.

The Radicalization Pipeline

Perhaps the most concerning aspect of escapism through hidden networks is its potential to facilitate radicalization. The same psychological mechanisms that make hidden networks attractive for identity exploration and community building can also draw individuals into extremist ideologies and criminal activities.

The radicalization process in hidden networks typically begins with legitimate grievances or psychological needs. Individuals seeking understanding, purpose, or belonging find communities that initially appear to offer these things. Gradually, through exposure to increasingly extreme content and social pressure from community members, their worldviews shift toward more radical positions.

The psychology of this transformation reveals how normal cognitive biases can be manipulated in hidden environments. Confirmation bias leads users to seek information that supports their developing beliefs while avoiding contradictory evidence. Social proof mechanisms encourage conformity with community norms, even as those norms drift toward extremism. The echo chamber effect, enhanced by the self-selecting nature of hidden communities, reinforces radical ideas through constant repetition and validation.

The anonymity and perceived safety of hidden networks accelerate radicalization by reducing social constraints on extreme thinking. Ideas that would be immediately challenged in conventional social settings can develop and spread unchecked in anonymous communities. Users may express increasingly radical views as a way of gaining status and acceptance within these groups.

Understanding this radicalization process is crucial for comprehending the broader psychological ecology of hidden networks. The same features that make these spaces valuable for legitimate privacy and community needs also make them vulnerable to exploitation by extremist movements and criminal organizations.

Concluding Thoughts: The Human Element in Digital Shadows

The psychology of hidden users reveals the hidden web not merely as a technological space but as a fundamentally human one, shaped by the same drives, needs, and vulnerabilities that characterize all human social organization. Fear, greed, and the desire for power provide the initial motivation for entering anonymous networks, but it is the complex interplay of community dynamics, identity exploration, and escapist needs that sustains long-term engagement with these systems.

The communities that emerge in hidden networks demonstrate both the resilience and fragility of human social bonds. Despite the absence of traditional identity markers and authority structures, users create elaborate systems of trust, reputation, and social organization. Yet these communities remain vulnerable to the same forces that threaten all human relationships betrayal, conflict, and the corrosive effects of fear and suspicion.

The escapist dimensions of hidden networks reveal both their greatest promise and their most significant danger. For individuals genuinely threatened by persecution or seeking support for stigmatized experiences, anonymous networks can provide life-saving resources and communities. However, the same features that make these spaces valuable for legitimate purposes also make them attractive to those seeking to exploit, manipulate, or radicalize others.

Understanding the psychology of hidden users is essential for anyone seeking to address the challenges posed by anonymous networks. Technical solutions alone, whether enhanced cybersecurity measures or improved law enforcement capabilities cannot address the underlying human needs and motivations that sustain hidden communities. Effective approaches must acknowledge both the legitimate functions these networks serve and the genuine psychological benefits they provide to their users.

The hidden web thus serves as a mirror, reflecting not only our fears and desires but our fundamental need for connection, understanding, and agency in an increasingly complex and monitored world. As technology continues to evolve and the boundaries between digital and physical reality continue to blur, understanding these psychological dynamics becomes ever more crucial for navigating the shadows that exist alongside our illuminated digital lives.

In the next chapter, we will explore how these individual psychological dynamics intersect with larger geopolitical forces. We will examine the role of state actors in hidden networks, where personal motivations converge with national interests, transforming spaces of individual escape into arenas of global conflict. Here, the psychology of the hidden user becomes entangled with the ambitions of nations, creating new forms of warfare fought entirely in the digital shadows.

CHAPTER FIVE

State Actors and Cyber Warfare

Throughout history, espionage has been a constant in the power struggles between nations. Spies infiltrated courts, intercepted letters, and bribed informants in the quest for intelligence. The Great Game between Britain and Russia in the 19th century, the elaborate networks of World War II, and the cat-and-mouse games of the Cold War all demonstrate humanity's enduring need to peer into the secrets of rivals. But in the digital age, the arena of espionage has expanded into a new dimension: cyberspace. Here, state actors exploit the shadows of the cloud to gather secrets, disrupt adversaries, and project influence without ever crossing a physical border. The rise of hidden networks and encrypted platforms has given espionage new tools and reach, creating a battlefield where distance is irrelevant and stealth is absolute.

Traditional espionage required physical presence, meticulous planning, and significant human resources. An operative needs months or years to establish cover, build relationships, and gain access to sensitive information. The risks were enormous capture meant imprisonment, torture, or death. Intelligence agencies invested heavily in training programs, safe houses, and elaborate communication systems using dead drops, coded messages, and face-to-face meetings in shadowy corners of foreign cities.

Digital espionage has fundamentally transformed this paradigm. State-sponsored hackers can infiltrate systems thousands of miles away, exfiltrating classified documents, industrial blueprints, or political communications from the comfort of secure facilities in their home countries. A single keystroke can unlock more secrets than a traditional spy might gather in a lifetime. Unlike conventional spies, these digital operatives leave no footprints in foreign soil, complicating attribution and accountability. What once demanded networks of human informants can now be achieved by a handful of skilled cyber operatives, hidden behind layers of anonymity and technical obfuscation.

The scale and speed of digital espionage dwarf traditional methods. Where a human spy might photograph a handful of documents during a covert operation, a cyber intrusion can copy terabytes of data in minutes. The 2015 breach of the U.S. Office of Personnel Management, attributed to Chinese state actors, compromised the personal information of over 22 million federal employees and contractors. Such a comprehensive intelligence coup would have been impossible through conventional espionage methods, requiring thousands of human assets and decades of patient work.

Hidden networks amplify these operations exponentially. Darknet forums, encrypted marketplaces, and covert communication channels provide both infrastructure and cover for intelligence gathering. These platforms offer more than just anonymity; they provide access to a global ecosystem of criminal expertise and tools. States may exploit criminal communities, purchasing stolen data, zero-day exploits, malware kits, or access credentials from shadowy vendors who operate with impunity in these spaces. Others may disguise their operatives as ordinary users, blending into the digital crowds to coordinate attacks, recruit assets, or spread carefully crafted misinformation campaigns.

The commoditization of cybercrime tools on hidden networks has democratized espionage capabilities. Advanced persistent threat (APT) frameworks, once the exclusive domain of well-funded intelligence agencies, can now be purchased or rented on underground markets. This accessibility allows smaller nations or even non-state actors to punch above their weight in the intelligence game. By operating in these spaces, state actors can mask their involvement, making their actions indistinguishable from those of private criminals, hacktivist groups, or opportunistic cyber mercenaries.

The psychological warfare dimension of espionage has also expanded dramatically in the digital realm. Information warfare has become as important as the information itself. Leaked documents, fabricated narratives, and strategically staged cyberattacks can destabilize public trust in governments, corporations, or democratic institutions. The release of stolen emails during election cycles, the strategic timing of data breaches to coincide with sensitive negotiations, or the careful orchestration of information leaks to discredit political opponents all represent sophisticated psychological operations that leverage digital espionage capabilities.

In some cases, state actors weaponize stolen information not merely to exploit it for intelligence purposes but to release it strategically, eroding confidence in rivals and shaping public opinion. The art lies not just in stealing secrets but in determining when, where, and how to reveal them for maximum impact. Hidden networks become the staging ground for these operations, where documents can surface anonymously through seemingly independent sources, claims can be made without immediate verification, and narratives can take root in public consciousness before fact-checkers or authorities can respond effectively.

The attribution problem in cyber espionage creates a unique strategic advantage for state actors. Unlike traditional espionage, where captured operatives could be interrogated and diplomatic protests filed, cyber operations exist in a gray zone of plausible deniability. Technical forensics can provide circumstantial evidence of state involvement, but rarely the smoking gun that traditional espionage might leave behind. This ambiguity allows nations to operate more aggressively in cyberspace while maintaining diplomatic relationships and avoiding the consequences that would follow conventional espionage activities.

In this new era of espionage beyond borders, the shadows of the cloud are no longer just hiding places for criminals; they are strategic assets for nations seeking competitive advantage in an interconnected world. They offer states both operational cover and political deniability, enabling them to pursue intelligence objectives that would be impossible or prohibitively risky in conventional arenas. The challenge for defenders is not only to secure systems against technical intrusion but also to discern where the line between independent cybercriminals and state-backed operatives truly lies, a distinction that often proves both crucial and elusive.

Digital Battlefields and Proxy Conflicts

As cyberspace has matured from a research curiosity into the backbone of modern civilization, it has become clear that it is not merely an extension of the physical world but a battlefield in its own right. Nations now recognize cyber capabilities as essential components of military strategy, alongside traditional domains of land, sea, air, and space. Military academies teach cyber warfare doctrine, defense departments establish dedicated cyber commands, and national security strategies explicitly acknowledge cyberspace as a domain of conflict. Yet, unlike conventional warfare, cyber conflicts rarely unfold as direct confrontations between clearly identified adversaries. Instead, they play out in the shadows, through proxy actors, covert operations, and asymmetric tactics designed to exploit vulnerabilities while avoiding the escalation dynamics that govern traditional military conflicts.

Digital battlefields are defined not by geographic territory or strategic chokepoints but by critical infrastructure: power grids that keep cities running, financial systems that process trillions of dollars in transactions, communication networks that connect billions of people, healthcare facilities that safeguard public health, transportation systems that move goods and people, and even democratic institutions like voting systems that legitimize governments. By targeting these digital arteries of modern society, state actors can weaken adversaries without firing a single shot or crossing a single border.

The strategic calculus of cyber warfare differs fundamentally from conventional military thinking. A well-timed cyberattack can paralyze entire economic sectors, sow chaos in society, and undermine public confidence in leadership and institutions. The 2007 cyber-attacks on Estonia demonstrated how digital assaults could effectively shut down a modern connected society, disrupting everything from banking and telecommunications to government services and media outlets. The incident served as a wake-up call for nations worldwide, illustrating how cyber weapons could achieve strategic effects traditionally associated with conventional military campaigns.

Unlike kinetic weapons such as bombs or missiles, cyber weapons can strike invisibly and often without immediate detection. Sophisticated malware can lurk in systems for months or years, gathering intelligence or positioning for future attacks. The Stuxnet worm, discovered in 2010, had reportedly been active for years before its detection, quietly sabotaging Iran's nuclear enrichment program while appearing to function normally. This stealth capability fundamentally alters the tempo and character of conflict, allowing adversaries to achieve strategic objectives while victims remain unaware, they are under attack.

The attribution challenge in cyberspace creates unique opportunities for proxy conflicts. Rather than engaging directly and risking diplomatic or military escalation, nations often rely on affiliated hacker groups, criminal syndicates, or ideologically aligned actors to carry out operations on their behalf. This outsourcing provides both enhanced capability and crucial plausible deniability. A nationalist hacker collective may launch attacks that align perfectly with their sponsor nation's strategic interests, while the sponsoring state maintains the fiction of non-involvement and even condemns the attacks through official channels.

These proxy relationships exist along a spectrum of control and coordination. At one end, states may directly fund and coordinate with criminal groups, providing them with intelligence, resources, and protection in exchange for conducting specific operations. At the other extreme, states may simply create permissive environments where aligned actors can operate freely, knowing that their activities will serve broader national interests even without explicit coordination. Hidden networks serve as the connective tissue for these relationships, providing secure communication channels, resource sharing, and operational coordination under multiple layers of anonymity.

The asymmetric nature of cyber warfare makes it especially attractive to smaller nations and non-state actors seeking to challenge more powerful adversaries. Unlike traditional arms races, where industrial capacity, population size, and economic resources largely determine military potential, cyber warfare rewards ingenuity, stealth, technical expertise, and adaptability over raw resources. A small team of talented hackers operating from a modest facility can potentially inflict damage on a superpower's critical infrastructure that would previously have required massive conventional military forces.

Hidden forums and black markets further level the playing field by commoditizing sophisticated cyber weapons and techniques. Advanced malware frameworks, zero-day exploits, and tactical knowledge that once required years of development and millions of dollars in investment can now be purchased or rented on underground markets for relatively modest sums. This democratization allows even resource-limited states to access cyber capabilities that rival those of major powers, fundamentally altering the balance of power in international relations.

The psychological dimension of cyber conflicts cannot be overstated. Unlike conventional military campaigns that often aim for decisive battlefield victories, cyberattacks rarely seek to destroy infrastructure outright. Instead, they aim to destabilize, create uncertainty, and make societies question their security and resilience. The true target is often social cohesion and public confidence rather than specific military or economic assets.

Whether manifesting as ransomware attacks on hospitals that endanger public health, disruptions of financial services that threaten economic stability, or sophisticated disinformation campaigns that undermine democratic processes, cyber operations achieve strategic effects by creating fear, confusion, and doubt. The mere possibility of cyber-attack can change behavior, forcing adversaries to divert resources to defensive measures and creating a climate of uncertainty that complicates decision-making at all levels of society.

In this evolving landscape, digital battlefields are not confined to traditional war zones or military installations, they are everywhere. Any connected device, from smartphones to smart home appliances, any networked system from corporate databases to industrial control systems, and any online platform from social media to e-commerce sites can become a theater of conflict. Hidden networks magnify this ubiquitous threat by providing both the tools and the concealment necessary for state actors to wage war by other means, blurring the lines between peace and conflict, combatant and civilian, battlefield and daily life.

Clouds as Tools of National Power

To understand the trajectory of international relations in the 21st century, one must recognize that the cloud is no longer a neutral technological medium or simply a commercial platform for digital services. It has evolved into a fundamental instrument of national power, wielded by states to extend influence, assert technological sovereignty, project soft power, and safeguard strategic interests across borders. In the shadows of the cloud, nations are not merely passive observers or neutral facilitators; they are active architects, deliberately shaping the digital landscape to serve their geopolitical objectives and advance their position in an increasingly connected world.

The concept of data sovereignty has emerged as a cornerstone of modern statecraft. Control of data flows has become as strategically important as control of traditional geographic territories, shipping lanes, or energy resources. Nations that dominate cloud infrastructure through ownership of data centers, control of undersea cables, development of foundational platforms, and establishment of technical standards gain unprecedented leverage over the information flows that sustain modern societies and economies.

This dominance extends far beyond economic considerations to encompass fundamental questions of national security and geopolitical influence. Access to global data flows enables comprehensive surveillance capabilities, strategic intelligence gathering, and even subtle manipulation of information ecosystems. The ability to monitor, analyze, and potentially disrupt the communications and data of other nations provides strategic advantages that previous generations of leaders could hardly imagine. In this context, the cloud has become the new commanding heights of international competition, where technological control directly translates to geopolitical advantage.

State actors leverage cloud infrastructure to project soft power in increasingly sophisticated ways. By sponsoring platforms that emphasize privacy, encryption, and digital rights, they can attract dissidents, journalists, activists, and civil society organizations from around the world, subtly shaping global narratives and positioning themselves as champions of digital freedom. These platforms serve dual purposes: providing genuine services to users seeking privacy and security while simultaneously creating channels for influence and intelligence gathering.

Conversely, by infiltrating, disrupting, or manipulating rival platforms and services, states can erode trust in adversaries' technological capabilities and democratic institutions. The revelation that foreign intelligence services have compromised popular social media platforms, encrypted messaging services, or cloud storage providers can have profound effects on public confidence and user behavior, even when the actual security impact may be limited.

The duality of cloud services serving simultaneously as digital sanctuaries and potential weapons of influence makes them uniquely suited to the subtle arts of 21st-century statecraft. Unlike traditional instruments of power that operate through obvious displays of force or formal diplomatic channels, cloud-based influence operations can shape perceptions and behaviors while remaining largely invisible to their targets.

Cyber sovereignty has emerged as another critical front in the struggle for technological dominance. Some nations pursue strategies of digital isolationism, implementing strict controls over their domestic cloud infrastructure, restricting foreign technology companies' operations, and ensuring that sensitive data remains within national borders under domestic legal frameworks. These approaches prioritize security and control over efficiency and innovation, reflecting concerns about foreign surveillance, economic espionage, and political manipulation.

Other nations adopt expansionist approaches, actively pursuing global influence by embedding their technology in international infrastructure, establishing overseas data centers, and promoting their platforms and standards worldwide. These strategies sacrifice some control and security for the potential to extend influence far beyond national borders, creating dependencies and gathering intelligence on a global scale.

The emergence of national cloud strategies reflects the recognition that technological infrastructure has become as strategically important as traditional military capabilities. Countries develop comprehensive plans for cloud development, complete with investment priorities, regulatory frameworks, and security requirements. These strategies often explicitly link technological capabilities to national security objectives, economic competitiveness, and geopolitical influence.

Hidden networks both complicate and amplify these power struggles by providing alternative channels that operate outside traditional regulatory and legal frameworks. Authoritarian regimes may use darknet services to circumvent international sanctions or surveillance, while democratic governments may leverage these same networks for intelligence operations or to support dissidents in repressive countries. The covert nature of these networks makes them attractive tools for pursuing objectives that cannot be achieved through conventional diplomatic or commercial channels.

The competition for cloud dominance has also sparked new forms of technological nationalism, with countries prioritizing domestic technology companies, restricting foreign investment in strategic sectors, and developing indigenous alternatives to foreign platforms and services. This trend reflects growing awareness that dependence on foreign technology infrastructure creates vulnerabilities that adversaries can exploit during times of tension or conflict.

Trade wars have increasingly focused on technology companies and cloud services, with nations using economic sanctions, regulatory restrictions, and diplomatic pressure to limit rivals' technological influence while promoting their own champions. The battle over 5G network infrastructure, restrictions on foreign cloud providers, and requirements for data localization all reflect this broader competition for technological dominance.

The militarization of cloud infrastructure represents another significant development in this domain. Military organizations worldwide are developing dedicated cloud capabilities, both for their own operations and as tools of cyber warfare. The ability to rapidly deploy computing resources, analyze vast amounts of intelligence data, and coordinate complex operations across global networks has become essential to modern military effectiveness.

The Evolution of Cyber Deterrence

The traditional concepts of deterrence, developed during the nuclear age, prove inadequate for addressing the unique characteristics of cyber conflict. Unlike nuclear weapons, which create obvious destruction and clear attribution, cyber weapons operate in a realm of ambiguity where effects can be subtle, delayed, or completely hidden. This ambiguity complicates efforts to establish effective deterrent relationships between states and creates opportunities for escalation and miscalculation.

The challenge of attribution in cyberspace fundamentally undermines classical deterrence theory, which depends on the ability to identify attackers and threaten proportional retaliation. When cyberattacks can be launched through multiple layers of proxies, technical obfuscation, and false flag operations, victim states often cannot determine with certainty who has attacked them, making targeted retaliation difficult or impossible.

The development of norms and rules for state behavior in cyberspace remains an ongoing process, with various international bodies, academic institutions, and government agencies working to establish frameworks that might reduce the risk of cyber conflicts while preserving legitimate defensive capabilities. However, the rapid pace of technological change often outpaces these diplomatic efforts, creating situations where new capabilities emerge faster than the rules governing their use.

State actors have fundamentally transformed the hidden web from a primarily criminal underworld into a strategic domain of global conflict and competition. Espionage operations that once required years of preparation and enormous human resources can now be conducted remotely by small teams of technical specialists. Proxy wars play out through networks of affiliated hackers and criminal organizations, allowing nations to pursue aggressive objectives while maintaining plausible deniability. The manipulation of cloud infrastructure and information flows has become a cornerstone of modern statecraft, enabling influence operations and intelligence gathering on unprecedented scales.

This transformation reflects broader changes in the nature of international conflict itself. Cyber warfare has systematically blurred the traditional distinctions between war and peace, soldier and civilian, and battlefield and daily life. The binary categories that governed previous eras of conflict combatant versus non-combatant, military versus civilian infrastructure, and wartime versus peacetime prove inadequate for understanding a domain where attacks can be launched from anywhere, target anything connected to the internet, and achieve strategic effects without crossing traditional thresholds of conflict.

To navigate this complex new environment, it is insufficient to focus solely on technical defensive measures like firewalls, encryption, and access controls, though these remain important elements of cybersecurity. Decision-makers must also develop sophisticated understanding of state strategies, national motivations, and the ways in which hidden networks serve as instruments of power projection and influence. The shadows of the digital realm are no longer merely personal refuges for privacy-seeking individuals or criminal havens for illicit commerce; they have become theaters of geopolitics where the balance of power in the 21st century is actively contested and shaped.

The implications extend beyond national security to encompass fundamental questions about democracy, privacy, economic competitiveness, and human rights in an interconnected world. As states become more sophisticated in their use of cyber capabilities, citizens, businesses, and civil society organizations must grapple with the reality that their digital lives are increasingly embedded within broader geopolitical struggles they may neither understand nor consent to participate in.

While encrypted platforms and privacy technologies offer significant protection against surveillance and tracking, the reality of digital anonymity is far more complex and fragile than most users realize. Understanding the technical, operational, and human factors that can compromise anonymity is essential for anyone seeking to understand both the vulnerabilities of hidden actors and the methods employed by those who pursue them across the digital realm.

CHAPTER SIX

The Illusion of Anonymity

For as long as humans have interacted online, the idea of vanishing into digital shadows has been intoxicating. The hidden web thrives on this allure, promising a cloak of invisibility to those who dare step beyond the surface. Forums, markets, and communities scattered across the dark corners of the internet promote themselves as sanctuaries of anonymity, offering users the freedom to speak, trade, and act without fear of consequence. Yet behind this promise lies an uncomfortable truth: anonymity is more fragile than it appears, and every step in the digital world leaves behind traces, however faint.

The internet was never designed to be anonymous. At its core, it is an immense communication system, one that requires every device to identify itself in order to send and receive information. IP addresses, connection logs, timestamps, metadata all of these form part of the invisible scaffolding of cyberspace. Tools like Tor, I2P, or VPNs attempt to obscure these identifiers, but they do not erase them. Instead, they complicate the trail, layering it with detours and obfuscation.

For skilled investigators, these trails are like tangled threads: difficult to follow, but not impossible to untangle.

What undermines anonymity most, however, is not the infrastructure of the internet but the fallibility of its users. Technical protections may be sophisticated, but humans are prone to error. A criminal who carefully routes traffic through multiple anonymizing layers might, in a moment of haste, log into a personal email from the same machine. A whistleblower might release a document without scrubbing its metadata, inadvertently revealing the username of their operating system. A fraudster may reuse the same pseudonym on both the dark web and a mainstream social network, linking their secret and public identities in a way that no encryption can undo.

Even the simple act of writing carries its own fingerprint. Linguists and computer scientists have developed stylometric tools capable of analyzing sentence structure, word choice, and punctuation patterns to identify authorship with startling accuracy. Forensic linguistics has unmasked anonymous bloggers, hackers, and activists, proving that anonymity can be undermined by nothing more than the quirks of human expression. In the hidden web, where pseudonyms abound, the unconscious habits of language can betray even the most careful actor.

Moreover, technical traces extend beyond direct actions. Time zones embedded in logs, software versions hidden in traffic, or recurring activity patterns can all serve as identifiers. Cybersecurity professionals routinely exploit these small details to narrow down suspects. If a forum administrator consistently logs in at 3 a.m. GMT, patterns can reveal both their geographic location and daily routine. A series of posts written in Cyrillic or Mandarin might reduce the field of suspects further. Anonymity is never absolute, it is an illusion crafted by tools and practices, vulnerable to cracks whenever users let their guard down.

This reality creates a paradox. The hidden web appears shrouded in secrecy, yet its participants constantly leave behind fragments of themselves. Each fragment is harmless in isolation, but together they form mosaics of identity. What is often mistaken for impenetrable anonymity is, in truth, a temporary veil, thin, patchy, and vulnerable to those with the patience to pull at their edges.

Law Enforcement in Pursuit

If anonymity is an illusion, then law enforcement has become the illusion's most determined challenger. Over the past two decades, police agencies, intelligence services, and cybersecurity units have evolved from outsiders in the digital realm to sophisticated hunters who navigate their complexities with ease. Their mission is not only to disrupt the most dangerous aspects of the hidden web but also to send a clear message: there are no perfect shadows online.

The takedown of Silk Road in 2013 is emblematic of this reality. For years, Silk Road had operated as the crown jewel of the darknet economy, a sprawling marketplace for narcotics, forged documents, and illicit services. Its founder,

Ross Ulbricht, known under the alias "Dread Pirate Roberts," believed his operation to be unassailable. The Tor network cloaked its servers, Bitcoin transactions disguised its finances, and a loyal community helped enforce order. Yet law enforcement agencies, working across jurisdictions, quietly pieced together his mistakes. An early post promoting the site was linked to an email address bearing Ulbricht's real name. Metadata, travel patterns, and slips in online behavior gradually narrowed the field. When agents finally arrested him in a San Francisco library, his laptop was still open to the marketplace's administrator dashboard; it was proof that even the most careful operators could not outrun persistence.

Silk Road was not an isolated victory. Law enforcement has dismantled dozens of darknet markets since then, often using undercover operations. Agents pose as buyers, sellers, or fellow administrators, slowly gaining trust within communities. Over time, they collect intelligence, map networks, and identify vulnerabilities. These undercover tactics mimic the slow burn of traditional organized crime investigations, where infiltrators build years-long cover stories. The difference is that in the digital realm, trust is fragile, and a single slip can unravel entire operations.

Technical innovation has also shifted the balance in favor of law enforcement. Blockchain analysis firms, often working hand-in-hand with investigators, have developed tools that can trace cryptocurrency transactions once thought untraceable. Every Bitcoin transaction leaves a permanent record on the blockchain. While these records do not reveal identities directly, patterns emerge when combined with real-world data. Criminals who convert illicit funds into fiat currency through regulated exchanges must eventually interact with systems that demand identification. Once this link is established, the entire web of their transactions becomes visible. The fall of AlphaBay, another massive darknet market, demonstrated how tracing financial flows can bring down seemingly untouchable empires.

Collaboration across borders is essential in this pursuit. Cybercrime is inherently global, and criminals often exploit jurisdictional gaps to hide. Recognizing this, agencies like Europol, Interpol, and the FBI have established dedicated cyber divisions that share intelligence and resources. Multi-country takedowns, such as Operation Onymous in 2014, demonstrated the power of collective action, shuttering dozens of hidden services in a single coordinated strike.

However, the growing power of law enforcement in the digital shadows raises ethical and political questions. The same techniques used to unmask drug lords or traffickers can also target whistleblowers, activists, or dissidents operating under oppressive regimes. Governments with authoritarian tendencies have seized on surveillance technologies to silence opposition, blurring the line between justice and repression. While Western agencies frame their actions as necessary to combat crime, critics warn that unchecked digital policing could erode privacy rights and stifle legitimate dissent.

Despite these concerns, the reality remains clear: law enforcement has shown that the promise of anonymity is far from absolute. The hidden web may delay detection, but it rarely guarantees it. For every operator who slips away undetected, many more find their veils of secrecy torn apart, their illusions of invisibility shattered by a combination of patience, technology, and human fallibility.

Famous Cases of Unmasking Shadows

History offers a catalog of stories that illustrate the fragility of digital anonymity. These stories are more than sensational headlines; they are cautionary tales, reminders that no amount of technical shielding can protect individuals from their own errors or from the relentless attention of determined investigators.

Perhaps no story looms larger than that of Ross Ulbricht. His rise as the mastermind behind Silk Road was matched only by the speed of his downfall. Despite his careful efforts, small errors accumulated: the reuse of a pseudonym, the careless mention of a philosophy unique to his personal beliefs, and the failure to fully separate his digital and real-world identities. These threads, invisible at first, eventually wove together into a map that led directly to him. His arrest marked not only the end of Silk Road but also the beginning of a new era of skepticism toward anonymity.

The takedown of "Playpen," a massive child exploitation forum, offers another example. In 2015, the FBI seized the site and, instead of immediately shutting it down, ran it for weeks as a sting operation. During this time, they deployed a "network investigative technique," essentially a form of malware, to identify thousands of users across the globe. What made the operation remarkable was not only its technical sophistication but also its sheer scale thousands of individuals who once believed themselves hidden were suddenly exposed. The case provoked fierce debate over legal boundaries and privacy, but it left little doubt that anonymity could be pierced when agencies were determined enough.

Even hacktivist collectives like Anonymous, which pride themselves on their ability to hide behind masks and pseudonyms, have seen their ranks infiltrated and exposed. Investigators tracked individuals through repeated mistakes: reusing usernames across forums, failing to mask time zones, or leaving identifiable linguistic signatures in their communications. The unmasking of high-profile members dealt blows to the group's mystique, proving that even the most coordinated anonymity is vulnerable to human weakness.

Cryptocurrency, too, has revealed its limits. The downfall of darknet markets like AlphaBay and Hansa was made possible by blockchain analysis. Investigators traced transactions across wallets, identifying administrators and major vendors who once thought their financial movements invisible. Each arrest chipped away at the myth that digital currencies could shield users indefinitely. Today, law enforcement openly boasts of its ability to trace blockchain transactions, a development that has reshaped how criminals attempt to launder funds.

Taken together, these cases underscore a sobering truth: anonymity is never total. It may delay discovery, and it may complicate investigations, but it cannot eliminate risk. The stories of unmasking serve as warnings to those who enter the shadows believing themselves untouchable. In reality, the shadows are porous, and the longer one lingers in them, the more likely it is that light will sweep in.

Anonymity is the lifeblood of the hidden web, but it is also its greatest illusion. It tempts individuals with promises of invisibility while concealing the cracks that make true secrecy impossible. Every digital action leaf behind echoes, every system is vulnerable to exploitation, and every human being is prone to error. Law enforcement, armed with persistence, collaboration, and ever-advancing technology, has demonstrated time and again that the illusion can be shattered.

For the whistleblower hiding from a repressive regime, these cracks in anonymity can be terrifying. For the trafficker, drug lord, or fraudster, they can mean the end of an empire. For society, they raise questions about how much privacy should be sacrificed in the name of security.

As we move forward into the next chapter, the focus shifts from the illusion of identity to the fuel that sustains hidden economies: money. Cryptocurrencies, once hailed as the perfect instruments of anonymous trade, are themselves subject to the same paradoxes as anonymity, promising invisibility while leaving behind indelible traces. In the dark economy, as in the hidden web at large, the shadows are never quite as opaque as they appear.

CHAPTER SEVEN

Cryptocurrencies and the Dark Economy

The Birth of Digital Money

The hidden economy that thrives beneath the surface web needed more than just anonymity of identity it needed a financial system capable of sustaining its clandestine operations. Traditional banking, with its regulatory oversight, centralized record keeping, and mandatory identification checks, was fundamentally incompatible with the ethos of secrecy that defined the dark web. Wire transfers or credit cards left paper trails, each transaction tethered to the individual behind it. For a thriving underground economy to take root, it required a currency that could operate outside of governments and banks. The arrival of Bitcoin in 2009 was therefore nothing short of revolutionary.

When Satoshi Nakamoto released the Bitcoin whitepaper, the promise was bold: a peer-to-peer electronic cash system that eliminated the need for trusted intermediaries. Instead of banks verifying transactions, a decentralized network of nodes would confirm and record them. Instead of centralized ledgers, a blockchain, a distributed, immutable record, would serve as the financial memory of the system. What was perhaps most radical was the idea that Bitcoin transactions, while recorded publicly, were pseudonymous. Wallets were identified not by names or IDs, but by long strings of alphanumeric characters. For those seeking liberation from surveillance, this anonymity seemed like a gift.

The timing could not have been more fortuitous. The world was reeling from the 2008 financial crisis, and trust in traditional banks was eroding. Activists, libertarians, and technophiles gravitated toward Bitcoin as a way of resisting centralized power. Yet beyond these idealists, another group saw enormous potential: operators in the hidden web. Silk Road, launched in 2011, became one of the first major platforms to embrace Bitcoin as its exclusive currency. For buyers and sellers alike, it offered a way to conduct business without the friction of banks or the prying eyes of regulators. Drugs, fake IDs, hacking tools, and even hitman services were priced in Bitcoin. Within two years, Silk Road was processing hundreds of millions of dollars' worth of transactions, and its model inspired dozens of imitators.

Bitcoin's success in this underground economy was built on two pillars: accessibility and perceived anonymity. Unlike earlier attempts at digital cash, Bitcoin required no centralized mint. Anyone with internet access could download a wallet and begin transacting. There were no borders, no exchange rates, and no approvals. Equally important was the belief, fostered both by enthusiasts and by early dark web adopters that Bitcoin was anonymous. For a time, this belief fueled explosive growth. Markets expanded, vendors multiplied, and Bitcoin became synonymous with the very idea of darknet commerce.

Yet Bitcoin's architecture carried within it a contradiction. Every transaction was permanently recorded on the blockchain. While wallet addresses did not carry names, the ledger itself was open to all, a transparent record of every coin that had ever moved. For years, this paradox went unnoticed or underappreciated. Criminals flocked to Bitcoin, convinced of its invisibility, unaware that each payment left indelible footprints waiting for the right tools to interpret them. The very feature that guaranteed Bitcoin's integrity, its transparency, would one day become its greatest weakness in the dark economy.

The Mechanics of the Underground Market

The dark economy is not merely a collection of illicit shops, it is a complex ecosystem with its own rules, hierarchies, and methods of operation. Cryptocurrencies became the bloodstream of this economy, pumping value across borders and between strangers who never met in person, who trusted neither governments nor each other. To understand how cryptocurrencies fueled this system, one must look at the mechanics that underpinned its daily function.

At the center of the dark economy are marketplaces, digital bazaars modeled after legitimate e-commerce platforms. Vendors advertise goods and services, complete with product descriptions, user reviews, and delivery guarantees. Buyers browse categories ranging from narcotics to counterfeit currency, from digital exploits to personal data. Cryptocurrencies facilitate these exchanges, often through escrow systems designed to build trust. A buyer deposits Bitcoin into the marketplace's escrow wallet; the funds are released to the vendor only once the goods are confirmed to have arrived. In theory, this structure reduces the risk of scams, creating a layer of reliability in an otherwise lawless space.

Around these marketplaces orbit smaller services, each tailored to solve specific challenges of operating in secrecy. Mixers, also known as tumblers, emerged as essential tools for laundering cryptocurrency. By pooling coins from multiple users and redistributing them in randomized amounts, mixers attempted to sever the trail of ownership. Criminals relied heavily on these services to mask the movement of funds, believing that the jumbling of coins rendered them untraceable. Similarly, decentralized exchanges allowed for the swapping of Bitcoin into privacy-focused currencies like Monero or Zcash, further complicating investigative efforts.

Vendors also invested in reputation as currency. A seller with thousands of positive reviews could command higher prices than a newcomer, just as trust on legitimate platforms like Amazon increases customer willingness to spend. Some vendors built entire brands, specializing in particular goods, say, high-purity narcotics or rare forged passports. Cryptocurrencies made this branding possible by enabling repeat transactions and long-term customer relationships. The anonymity of both sides meant reputation became the strongest form of identity.

The ecosystem extended beyond goods to services. Hackers offered malware kits for sale, complete with customer support and updates. DDoS-for-hire operations flourished, their payments seamlessly facilitated through crypto. Fraudsters sold credit card dumps by the thousands, each record priced in fractions of a coin. Even assassins and mercenaries claimed to accept payment in Bitcoin, though many of these offers were later revealed as scams. Cryptocurrency was the universal medium that bound together this chaotic array of commerce, ensuring that no matter what the service or product, payment could be executed quickly and across borders.

Yet beneath this thriving marketplace lay fragility. Market operators frequently turned to "exit scams," abruptly shutting down sites and vanishing with millions in escrowed cryptocurrency. Buyers and sellers alike were left empty-handed, a reminder that in a trustless economy, betrayal was always a risk. Similarly, law enforcement infiltrations, such as the simultaneous takedowns of AlphaBay and Hansa in 2017, revealed that even trusted platforms could be secretly controlled by investigators. In these instances, cryptocurrencies once again betrayed the illusion of invincibility escrowed. Bitcoin transactions became evidence, mixers failed to fully obscure trails, and blockchain analysis unraveled years of hidden commerce.

The dark economy thus evolved into a cat-and-mouse game. Criminals innovated with privacy coins, decentralized marketplaces, and peer-to-peer exchanges. Investigators responded with more sophisticated blockchain forensics, sting operations, and cross-border cooperation. The balance shifted back and forth, but one truth became clear: cryptocurrency was both the enabler and the vulnerability of the dark economy. It empowered underground trade on a scale previously impossible, yet it also created new avenues for exposure and accountability.

The Future of Crypto in the Shadows

As the dark economy matured, so did its relationship with cryptocurrency. Early reliance on Bitcoin gradually gave way to diversification. By the late 2010s, privacy-focused coins like Monero and Zcash gained prominence. Unlike Bitcoin, these currencies were designed to obscure transaction details. Monero, for instance, uses ring signatures and stealth addresses to make it virtually impossible to trace payments back to specific users. For many dark web operators, Monero became the currency of choice, with several marketplaces outright refusing to accept Bitcoin due to its traceability.

But the shift to privacy coins has not been without complications. Their relative obscurity makes them less liquid, harder to exchange for fiat currency, and less widely supported by exchanges. Many criminals still rely on Bitcoin because of its accessibility, even if it requires careful laundering. This tension between the convenience of Bitcoin and the privacy of alternatives defines much of the present landscape.

Looking ahead, cryptocurrencies in the dark economy are poised to evolve along two trajectories: innovation and adaptation. Innovation emerges from the development of new privacy technologies, such as zero-knowledge proofs, which allow transactions to be verified without revealing underlying details. Decentralized finance (DeFi) protocols also create opportunities for laundering funds in ever more sophisticated ways. Criminals exploit liquidity pools, flash loans, and decentralized exchanges to fragment and reassemble funds, leaving investigators struggling to follow.

Adaptation, on the other hand, reflects the response to growing law enforcement capabilities. Blockchain analysis firms are increasingly adept at tracing transactions, and regulators are tightening rules around exchanges. Criminals have adapted by turning to peer-to-peer platforms, where individuals trade cryptocurrencies directly without intermediaries. They use prepaid debit cards, gift cards, and even stable coins to move funds across borders. Some exploit gaps in regulation in countries with weak oversight, while others shift operations entirely into decentralized ecosystems.

Yet despite these innovations, the dark economy remains vulnerable to the same paradox that undermined anonymity: no system is perfect. Every cryptocurrency transaction leaves traces, whether through blockchain records, exchange interactions, or conversion points. For investigators, time is an ally. Transactions that appear opaque today may become transparent tomorrow as new analytical techniques emerge. What criminals see as impregnable walls often turn out to be temporary obstacles.

The larger question is whether cryptocurrency will always remain synonymous with the dark economy. While it is true that cryptocurrencies enabled the explosion of underground markets, they are also increasingly part of mainstream finance. Legitimate businesses accept Bitcoin, institutional investors hold it as an asset, and central banks are exploring their own digital currencies. This mainstreaming complicates the narrative, as cryptocurrencies become tools not only for criminals but also for everyday users, innovators, and financial institutions.

For the hidden web, this shift may prove to be both a blessing and a curse. On one hand, broader adoption normalizes cryptocurrency, making transactions less suspicious and harder to single out. On the other hand, mainstreaming brings regulation, oversight, and a flood of new forensic tools. The very success of cryptocurrencies as a global phenomenon may erode the secrecy that dark economies depend upon.

In the end, cryptocurrencies will likely remain entangled with the shadows of the web, even as they gain legitimacy elsewhere. They are the bridge that allowed the dark economy to flourish, and they will continue to serve as its lifeblood. But as history has shown, every tool of secrecy eventually becomes a tool of exposure. In the dance between anonymity and accountability, cryptocurrencies occupy both roles, fueling the shadows even as they illuminate them.

The story of cryptocurrencies in the dark economy is a story of duality. They empower individuals and markets to bypass centralized authority, offering freedom and financial sovereignty. At the same time, they empower criminals to exploit those freedoms, creating thriving ecosystems of illicit trade. Bitcoin's rise from obscure experiment to underground currency to mainstream financial asset captures this duality in stark relief.

For participants in the hidden web, cryptocurrencies are not merely tools of convenience, they are existential necessities. Without them, markets would collapse, vendors could not be paid, and trust between anonymous actors would evaporate. Yet the very features that make cryptocurrencies so powerful transparency, immutability, decentralization, also render them vulnerable to scrutiny. The blockchain never forgets, and in its permanence lies both strength and weakness.

As the hidden web continues to evolve, cryptocurrencies will remain central to its operation. But their role will be shaped not only by technological innovation but also by the relentless pursuit of those who seek to expose the shadows. The illusion of perfect anonymity, whether in identity or in finance, has always proven fragile. In the chapters that follow, we will examine how these shadows intersect with new frontiers of technology, from artificial intelligence to global surveillance systems, and ask whether true secrecy can ever exist in the digital age.

CHAPTER EIGHT

Artificial Intelligence in the Shadows

The Rise of Intelligent Shadows

Artificial Intelligence (AI) has become the defining technology of the twenty-first century, shaping industries, economies, and everyday life. From self-driving cars to personalized recommendations, from medical diagnostics to predictive policing, AI operates everywhere, often invisibly. Yet, as with every technological breakthrough, the same algorithms that empower progress also invite exploitation. Within the murky depths of the hidden web, AI has found a darker purpose. No longer confined to the laboratories of universities or the boardrooms of technology companies, AI now thrives in the shadows, where it serves as a weapon, a shield, and a force multiplier for cybercriminals, dissidents, and clandestine actors alike.

The hidden web has always thrived on asymmetry small groups leveraging technology to outmaneuver larger, better-funded adversaries. AI amplifies this imbalance. Tools that once required months of programming or specialized expertise can now be automated through machine learning models.

Tasks that demanded large teams can be executed by a single individual with access to pre-trained algorithms. For cybercriminals, AI represents efficiency; for dark markets, it represents sophistication; and for state-sponsored actors, it represents deniability.

One of the earliest and most visible uses of AI in the hidden spaces of the internet has been the automation of fraud. Machine learning models trained on stolen data can generate convincing fake identities, complete with realistic facial photos produced by generative adversarial networks (GANs). These synthetic personas can bypass identity verification systems, open bank accounts, or operate botnets disguised as legitimate users. The process of social engineering, once reliant on human intuition, is increasingly outsourced to AI-driven chatbots capable of mimicking natural conversation. Targets are manipulated with precision, their trust exploited with scripts that adapt in real time to responses.

Beyond fraud, AI plays a central role in the enhancement of cyberattacks. Algorithms can scan vast networks, identifying vulnerabilities faster than human analysts ever could. They can adapt malware signatures dynamically, mutating code to evade detection by antivirus programs. In distributed denial-of-service (DDoS) attacks, AI optimizes the deployment of botnets, allocating resources intelligently to overwhelm targets while minimizing exposure. The arms race between attackers and defenders has thus entered a new era: an era where algorithms battle algorithms in digital landscapes invisible to most.

But AI in the shadows is not solely about offense. It is also about defense and concealment. Dark web operators deploy AI systems to monitor their marketplaces, detecting potential infiltration by law enforcement or rival groups. Algorithms analyze user behavior patterns, flagging suspicious activity that might indicate an undercover agent. AI-driven moderation tools scrub forums of incriminating posts, ensuring that sensitive conversations remain beyond the reach of outsiders. In this way, artificial intelligence acts as both guardian and gatekeeper, preserving the integrity of the hidden ecosystems that depend on secrecy.

The rise of intelligent shadows reveals a sobering truth: AI is not inherently good or evil. It is a tool, and in the hands of those who dwell in the hidden web, it becomes a force that extends the boundaries of what is possible. Whether used to defraud, to protect, or to manipulate, AI has become as integral to the dark economy as cryptocurrencies before it. And just as Bitcoin reshaped the hidden marketplaces of the past decade, artificial intelligence is reshaping the threats and the opportunities that define the future.

Weaponizing Algorithms

Perhaps the most alarming dimension of AI in the shadows is its weaponization. While traditional cyberattacks have posed risks to businesses and governments, AI-driven attacks escalate the scale, precision, and unpredictability of these threats. Algorithms are tireless; they do not sleep, they do not forget, and they improve with every iteration. For those seeking to undermine digital infrastructures, AI transforms cybercrime from a craft into an industrialized process.

One of the most striking examples lies in deepfakes. Using neural networks, dark web actors can generate hyper-realistic videos of individuals saying or doing things they never did. At first, deepfakes were curiosities novelties shared for amusement. But their weaponization has opened chilling possibilities. False videos of political leaders making inflammatory statements can sow disinformation, destabilize governments, or manipulate elections. Pornographic deepfakes, often targeting women, have become tools of harassment, coercion, and exploitation. In underground forums, services for creating bespoke deepfakes are openly advertised, priced in cryptocurrency, and delivered within days. The power to distort reality, once reserved for Hollywood studios, is now available to anyone with the right connections in the shadows.

Phishing campaigns have also been supercharged by AI. Instead of generic, easily spotted scams, AI systems craft highly personalized messages based on scraped data from social media and stolen databases. These messages are tailored to individual targets, complete with personal references and linguistic quirks. Chatbots can carry out extended conversations, maintaining consistency in tone and style. Victims are drawn deeper into deception, convinced by the realism of the interaction. At scale, such campaigns blur the line between human and machine, leaving even vigilant users vulnerable.

Malware, too, has evolved under the influence of AI. Traditional malware relied on static code that could be identified and neutralized by security software. AI-powered malware, however, learns from its environment. It can analyze the defenses of a network, adapt its behavior to avoid detection, and even disguise itself as legitimate software. Some malware employs reinforcement learning, experimenting with different strategies until it identifies the most effective pathway for infiltration. In this sense, the malware becomes a living organism, evolving dynamically to outwit its prey.

Even more disturbing are autonomous cyber weapons programs capable of launching and sustaining attacks without human oversight. State actors have been rumored to develop AI-driven systems that can infiltrate critical infrastructure, lie dormant for years, and activate at the opportune moment. Imagine an algorithm designed to monitor a power grid, silently mapping vulnerabilities until it identifies the perfect time to trigger a blackout. Or consider an AI system capable of coordinating swarms of compromised devices, executing multi-pronged attacks against financial institutions. Such capabilities, once the stuff of science fiction, are rapidly becoming plausible within the hidden world of AI innovation.

The weaponization of algorithms underscores the asymmetric power of the hidden web. A single individual with access to advanced models can unleash chaos on a scale that once required entire armies of hackers. The democratization of AI tools is often open source and freely available ensures that the barrier to entry remains low. What separates a curious experimenter from a criminal mastermind is not access, but intent. And in the shadows, intent is rarely benign.

The Dual-Edged Future

As artificial intelligence embeds itself deeper into the hidden web, the question arises: what does the future hold? Will AI push the boundaries of crime and deception to new extremes, or will it ultimately illuminate the very shadows it now inhabits? The answer, as always, lies in the double-edged nature of technology.

On one side, AI promises even greater sophistication for dark web operators. The integration of AI with cryptocurrencies could lead to fully automated black markets, where bots negotiate prices, manage logistics, and deliver digital goods without human involvement. Imagine a marketplace where every vendor is an algorithm, every buyer a script, and every transaction executed through smart contracts. Such a system would reduce the vulnerabilities associated with human error, making infiltration by law enforcement exponentially more difficult.

Privacy-focused AI tools also loom on the horizon. Already, researchers are developing systems that can anonymize digital behavior in real time, masking the patterns that investigators rely on for attribution. Combined with encryption and decentralized networks, these tools could create nearly invisible communication channels. For dissidents and activists living under repressive regimes, such tools might offer lifesaving protection. For criminals, they represent near-total impunity.

Yet, the same intelligence that empowers secrecy also enables exposure. Law enforcement and cybersecurity firms are increasingly turning to AI for their own operations. Machine learning models analyze blockchain transactions, identify anomalies in network traffic, and predict potential cyberattacks before they occur. Natural language processing allows investigators to monitor dark web forums, extracting insights from coded slang and obscure dialects. Facial recognition systems scan images, identifying suspects even when they attempt to obscure their features. In this battle of algorithms, each side learns from the other, creating an accelerating feedback loop of innovation.

Perhaps the most profound implication lies in the erosion of trust. In an age where AI can fabricate identities, alter voices, and create fake evidence, the very concept of truth becomes fragile. Institutions, media, and individuals face the constant threat of manipulation, unsure of what to believe. In the hidden web, where deception is already currency, AI accelerates this collapse of certainty. The result is a digital landscape where trust must be continually verified, and where even verification itself can be faked.

The dual-edged future of AI in the shadows is therefore not merely a technical issue; it is an existential one. It challenges the boundaries of law, ethics, and perception. It forces us to confront uncomfortable realities: that machines can outthink us in deception, that truth can be manufactured at scale, and that secrecy is both weapon and shield. The hidden web has always thrived on ambiguity, but with AI, that ambiguity becomes nearly impenetrable.

Artificial intelligence in the shadows is more than a technological shift; it is a paradigm change. It redefines what is possible for those operating outside the boundaries of law and transparency. From generating identities to conducting autonomous attacks, from defending marketplaces to distorting reality itself, AI reshapes the hidden web into something more dynamic, more resilient, and more dangerous than ever before.

But this story is not one of inevitability. Just as AI empowers the shadows, it also equips those who fight against them. Algorithms illuminate patterns invisible to humans, uncovering the traces that criminals leave behind. Machine learning systems, trained on terabytes of dark web data, reveal trends that help predict and prevent crime. The same intelligence that fuels deception can also fuel detection. The shadows are intelligent, yes but intelligence cuts both ways.

What remains clear is that artificial intelligence is no longer confined to the visible internet or the realm of corporations. It has migrated into the hidden layers, embedding itself in markets, forums, and clandestine operations. Its influence is pervasive, its potential immense, and its risks profound. As we navigate the threats beyond the surface web, we must recognize that the battle is no longer human versus human; it is machine versus machine, algorithm versus algorithm, and shadow versus light.

The age of intelligent shadows has arrived, and its story is only beginning.

CHAPTER NINE

Global Surveillance and Resistance

The modern world is built upon networks of communication, commerce, transportation, and governance. Yet underlying these systems is another network, quieter and less visible: the architecture of surveillance. Every email sent, every message shared, and every transaction made generates data, and where there is data, there is the possibility of observation. Governments and corporations alike have constructed vast infrastructures to capture, store, and analyze this information. The result is a world where visibility is not just a byproduct of digital life but its defining feature.

Global surveillance has its roots in necessity. Nations have long sought to monitor adversaries, prevent attacks, and maintain control over their populations. The Cold War gave rise to signals intelligence programs such as ECHELON, where allied states intercepted communications across the globe. But the digital revolution of the twenty-first century magnified this capacity beyond measure. With smartphones in every pocket, sensors in every city, and satellites orbiting overhead, surveillance is no longer episodic but continuous. The question is not whether one is observed but how often, by whom, and to what end.

The revelations of Edward Snowden in 2013 peeled back the curtain on the true extent of this system. Programs such as PRISM exposed the collaboration between intelligence agencies and major technology companies, where user data was siphoned from servers and channeled to government analysts. Metadata, the who, when, and where of communication, proved just as valuable as content. Vast databases allowed governments to map relationships, detect patterns, and anticipate behaviors with unsettling precision. Even those with nothing to hide became part of a system where every action was logged, every interaction archived, and every move traceable.

Yet surveillance is not confined to governments. Corporations, too, have become powerful watchers. Tech giants harvest behavioral data to fuel targeted advertising, creating detailed psychological profiles of billions of users. Social media platforms track clicks, likes, and pauses to predict desires before they are consciously felt. Wearables monitor health, location, and daily routines, often without explicit consent. In this economy of surveillance capitalism, visibility is monetized, and privacy is the price of participation. The distinction between commercial monitoring and national security blurs as corporations share data with governments, willingly or under compulsion.

For many, this level of observation is justified under the promise of safety or convenience. Terrorist plots are foiled, diseases tracked, and crimes predicted. Yet the same architecture that protects can also repress. Authoritarian regimes harness surveillance to silence dissent, monitor activists, and control populations with unprecedented efficiency. From facial recognition systems in public squares to AI-powered monitoring of online speech, surveillance becomes a tool of power, a digital panopticon where the possibility of being watched shapes behavior. The shadows of the cloud are illuminated not by curiosity but by scrutiny, and resistance emerges as a natural response to overreach.

The Anatomy of Resistance

Surveillance may appear totally, but it is never absolute. For every system of observation, there arises a countermovement a strategy of concealment, disruption, or defiance. Resistance to global surveillance takes many forms, from individual acts of digital hygiene to collective efforts of technological innovation and political advocacy. These resistances are not merely reactive; they are proactive efforts to reclaim autonomy in a world where visibility is coerced.

Encryption has long been the cornerstone of resistance. By transforming messages into unreadable code, encryption ensures that even if communications are intercepted, their contents remain secure. Tools like Pretty Good Privacy (PGP), once confined to niche communities, have become essential for journalists, activists, and whistleblowers operating under threat. Encrypted messaging apps such as Signal and

WhatsApp now serve billions, offering end-to-end encryption that shields conversations from prying eyes. Though governments often decry such tools as barriers to law enforcement, for those in repressive environments, they are lifelines of safety.

Anonymity networks represent another layer of resistance. The Tor network, initially developed with support from the U.S. Navy, enables users to mask their location and identity by routing traffic through multiple relays. This system makes it difficult for observers to trace the origin of activity, creating safe spaces for free expression and access to censored information. Virtual Private Networks (VPNs) similarly obscure digital footprints, though their reliability depends on jurisdiction and provider. In places where internet access is heavily restricted, such as Iran or China, circumvention tools provide the only pathways to uncensored information.

But resistance is not limited to technical tools. It also manifests in culture and practice. The movement for digital rights, championed by organizations like the Electronic Frontier Foundation, challenges surveillance through legal advocacy, public education, and policy reform. Whistleblowers risk their freedom to expose abuses, as Snowden did with the NSA or Chelsea Manning with U.S. military records. Hacktivist groups disrupt surveillance systems directly, leaking documents, defacing websites, or launching denial-of-service attacks. For these actors, resistance is both a moral stance and a form of digital insurgency.

Even ordinary users engage in micro-resistance, consciously or unconsciously. They adjust privacy settings, block cookies, or limit their online presence. They use pseudonyms, disable location tracking, or migrate to platforms that prioritize security. While these actions may seem small, collectively they represent a cultural pushback against the normalization of surveillance. Each decision to obscure, to refuse, or to resist contributes to a broader atmosphere of defiance. The anatomy of resistance, then, is as diverse as the systems it opposes, technological, political, cultural, and personal.

Yet resistance is not without its risks. Encryption draws suspicion; anonymity can attract surveillance rather than deter it. Activists using circumvention tools risk detection, arrest, or worse. States develop increasingly sophisticated methods to undermine these protections, such as deploying AI to detect encrypted traffic patterns or infiltrating networks with compromised nodes. In this sense, resistance is a continual struggle a cat-and-mouse game where victories are temporary, and the stakes are high. But the very persistence of this struggle underscores a fundamental truth: surveillance may be powerful, but it is never uncontested.

The Future of Visibility and Defiance

The contest between surveillance and resistance defines the present, but it also shapes the future. As technology advances, both watchers and the watches evolve, developing new tactics to outmaneuver one another. The trajectory of this struggle will determine the contours of privacy, freedom, and power in the decades to come.

Emerging technologies promise to expand surveillance even further. Artificial intelligence, already deployed for facial recognition and behavioral analysis, will grow more sophisticated. Predictive algorithms may not only observe actions but anticipate them, categorizing individuals as risks before they act. Biometric monitoring through gait recognition, voice patterns, and even emotional cues will add new dimensions to visibility. Satellite constellations, drone swarms, and ubiquitous sensors will render the physical world as transparent as the digital. In such a landscape, invisibility may seem impossible.

Yet resistance adapts as well. Advances in cryptography, such as homomorphic encryption, promise secure computation without revealing underlying data. Decentralized technologies, from blockchain-based communication platforms to peer-to-peer networks, reduce reliance on centralized intermediaries vulnerable to surveillance. Research into adversarial machine learning demonstrates that AI systems can be tricked or blinded by carefully designed inputs. Activists experiment with clothing, makeup, and accessories that confuse facial recognition, transforming fashion into a form of resistance. The same ingenuity that fuels surveillance fuels counter-surveillance, ensuring that the future remains contested rather than predetermined.

On a political level, the debate over surveillance and privacy continues to intensify. In democratic societies, citizens demand accountability, pressing governments to limit overreach and regulate corporate data practices. The

European Union's General Data Protection Regulation (GDPR) represents one such effort, establishing legal frameworks to protect individual rights in the digital age. In contrast, authoritarian regimes double down on surveillance, embedding it into governance itself. The divergence between open and closed societies may hinge on their relationship to visibility, whether surveillance serves the people or subjugates them.

Perhaps the most profound question concerns trust. In a world where surveillance is pervasive, can individuals trust their governments, their technologies, or even their communities? Resistance often emerges from mistrust of abuse, of exploitation, of manipulation. For trust to be restored, transparency must flow both ways. Citizens must know not only that they are watched but also why, how, and with what safeguards. Without this reciprocity, resistance will remain a defining feature of the digital landscape.

The future of visibility and defiance, then, is not binary. It is not a question of total surveillance or total freedom. Rather, it is a dynamic equilibrium a shifting balance of power shaped by technology, law, and culture. The shadows of the cloud will always be contested space, where watchers and resisters move in tandem, each adapting to the other. The question is not whether this struggle will continue, but what kind of world it will produce: one where visibility empowers or one where it oppresses.

Global surveillance and resistance are two sides of the same coin, each defined by the other. Surveillance thrives on visibility; resistance thrives on invisibility. One seeks to know, the other to conceal. Yet this struggle is not static; it is a living contest, evolving with every technological advance and every political shift.

In examining this dynamic, we see not only the risks but also the possibilities. Surveillance can protect, but it can also repress. Resistance can liberate, but it can also endanger it. Both are necessary, in their own ways, to shape a world where power is balanced and freedom preserved. The challenge lies in ensuring that surveillance serves the collective good rather than domination and that resistance remains a tool of justice rather than chaos.

The story of global surveillance and resistance is, ultimately, the story of human agency in the digital age. It is about the choices we make about what to reveal, what to conceal, what to accept, and what to resist. The shadows of the cloud may be vast, but within them lies the potential for both control and freedom. The future depends on how we navigate this duality and on whether resistance can remain strong enough to keep the watchers in check.

CHAPTER TEN

Toward a Safer Digital Future

The twenty-first century has been defined by connectivity. Every aspect of human life communication, commerce, healthcare, governance, and even identity itself has migrated into the digital sphere. This transformation has brought profound opportunities, yet it has also introduced unprecedented vulnerabilities. The challenges described throughout this book cybercrime, surveillance, disinformation, and the shadow economies lurking beneath the surface web underscore the urgent need to rethink what security means in this era. To move toward a safer digital future, we must first reimagine security not as a static condition but as a living ecosystem, shaped by human behavior, technological innovation, and evolving threats.

Traditionally, security has been understood in terms of barriers and fortifications: firewalls, passwords, locks, and access controls. While these remain essential, they are insufficient in a world where threats are fluid and often invisible. Cybersecurity can no longer rely on keeping intruders out; instead, it must emphasize resilience, adaptability, and trust. This requires recognizing that perfect security is an illusion. Attacks will happen, breaches will occur, and systems will fail. The measure of safety lies not in preventing all harm but in minimizing impact, recovering quickly, and ensuring that no single failure cascades into catastrophe.

Resilience begins with architecture. Cloud infrastructures, supply chains, and critical systems must be designed with redundancy and failover capabilities. Networks must be segmented to prevent lateral movement, and sensitive data must be encrypted both in storage and in transit. But resilience is not purely technical. It also depends on people and cultures of awareness, transparency, and accountability. Organizations that treat security as a shared responsibility, rather than a burden of IT departments, are better positioned to withstand attacks. Individuals who practice good digital hygiene, strong authentication, careful sharing, and skepticism of suspicious activity form the human firewall that technology alone cannot provide.

Beyond resilience, a safer digital future demands an ethical reorientation of technology itself. The systems that shape our lives are not neutral; they embody the values of their creators and operators. When algorithms prioritize engagement over accuracy, misinformation spreads. When platforms monetize visibility, surveillance capitalism thrives. When governments pursue control over liberty, surveillance morphs into repression. Building safer futures requires embedding human rights, privacy, and dignity into the DNA of technological design. Security, in this sense, is not only about defense against attackers but also about defense against exploitation and abuse.

This rethinking of security extends across borders. The internet is global, but governance is fragmented, shaped by national laws, corporate policies, and cultural norms. A safer future will require collaborative frameworks, international agreements, industry standards, and cross-sector partnerships that transcend boundaries. Just as climate change demands a collective response, so too does cybersecurity. No single nation, company, or community can address threats that are inherently borderless. A global architecture of security, rooted in shared principles and mutual accountability, must replace the patchwork of isolated efforts. Without this reimagining, the shadows of the cloud will continue to expand, unchecked and unchallenged.

Innovation as Shield and Sword

The tools of tomorrow will determine whether the digital future is one of safety or peril. Innovation has always been double-edged: the same technology that empowers can also endanger. Artificial intelligence, quantum computing, blockchain, and biotechnology promise transformative benefits, yet they also present new risks. To build a safer digital future, societies must learn to wield innovation as both a shield and a sword, protecting against threats while enabling progress.

Artificial intelligence is already embedded in cybersecurity, powering systems that detect anomalies, predict attacks, and automate defenses. Machine learning can sift through vast datasets to identify patterns invisible to human analysts, allowing for faster and more accurate responses. Yet AI also powers the very threats it defends against: deepfakes that erode trust, automated hacking tools that scale attacks, and surveillance systems that track populations with unprecedented precision. The future of AI will depend on governance ensuring transparency. accountability, and ethical application. Rather than banning AI in security contexts, societies must channel its power toward defense while placing guardrails against its misuse.

Quantum computing presents both peril and promise. When mature, quantum machines could shatter current encryption systems, rendering vast troves of data vulnerable. But quantum technologies also hold the key to next-generation security, with quantum key distribution offering theoretically unbreakable communication. Preparing for this future requires foresight: developing post-quantum cryptography, investing in research, and ensuring that critical infrastructure is not caught unprepared. The race to quantum security is not optional; it is essential for survival in a world where information is power.

Blockchain and decentralization also play roles in building safer systems. Distributed ledgers reduce reliance on centralized authorities vulnerable to attack or abuse, enabling trust through mathematics rather than institutions. In finance, blockchain has enabled cryptocurrencies, both empowered individuals and fueling dark economies. Yet its potential extends further: secure supply chains, transparent voting systems, and decentralized identity management. By anchoring trust in decentralized networks, societies may build infrastructures resistant to both cyberattack and centralized overreach. The challenge lies in balancing decentralization with usability, ensuring that systems remain accessible without sacrificing their integrity.

Biotechnology introduces another frontier of security. As health data moves online and bioinformatics advances, the line between biological and digital vulnerabilities blurs. Cyberattacks on medical infrastructure, genetic databases, or bioengineering platforms could have consequences far beyond the digital realm. A safer digital future will require integrating cybersecurity with biosecurity, ensuring that as humans engineer life itself, they also safeguard it from malicious interference.

Innovation is neither inherently good nor bad. It reflects human intent. The safer digital future depends on shaping innovation through deliberate choices: designing systems with privacy by default, building transparency into algorithms, and aligning technological development with social good. Just as fire can warm or destroy, technology can protect or imperial. Harnessing it as a shield rather than a sword is the responsibility of creators, regulators, and users alike.

Toward Collective Stewardship

If the digital future is to be safer, it cannot be left to chance, nor can it be entrusted to isolated actors. Governments alone cannot safeguard cyberspace, nor can corporations, nor can individuals. The task demands collective stewardship, a recognition that the digital commons belongs to all and that all must share in its protection.

Governments have a critical role in establishing legal frameworks and protecting critical infrastructure. Yet they must balance this responsibility with respect for rights. Overreach risks turning security into control, while underreach leaves citizens vulnerable. International cooperation will be key, particularly in developing treaties and norms to govern cyber conflict, regulate surveillance, and prevent weaponization of emerging technologies. Just as nuclear arms control required global agreement, so too will cyber peace demand shared commitments. Without such frameworks, the digital future risks becoming a battleground rather than a common.

Corporations, as the custodians of much of the world's data and infrastructure, bear unique responsibility. They must design systems that prioritize user safety, resist exploitation, and minimize data collection. Transparency in data practices, accountability for breaches, and commitment to ethical AI are not optional but fundamental. Profit cannot be allowed to eclipse responsibility. Companies that treat users as commodities erode trust and contribute to the very instability they claim to prevent. In contrast, corporations that embed stewardship into their models will shape markets, societies, and futures in profound ways.

Civil society and individuals, too, must be active stewards. Digital literacy is as essential today as reading and writing were in past centuries. Understanding the basics of privacy, security, and information hygiene empowers individuals to protect themselves and their communities. Activists, journalists, and advocacy groups amplify these efforts, ensuring that public discourse holds governments and corporations accountable. Resistance, as discussed in the previous chapter, is part of stewardship it ensures that surveillance and exploitation are not left unchallenged.

Education will play a pivotal role. A safer digital future requires generational change in how societies understand technology. Children must grow up with awareness of their digital footprints, the value of privacy, and the importance of critical thinking in the face of misinformation. Universities must integrate ethics into computer science curricula, ensuring that the next generation of engineers considers not just what they can build, but what they should. Public campaigns must raise awareness about security practices, bridging the gap between experts and everyday users.

Collective stewardship also means recognizing the interconnectedness of threats. Cyberattacks on hospitals are not only technical issues; they are human crises. Disinformation campaigns are not only political problems; they are societal fractures. Surveillance is not only a tool of states; it is a force that shapes culture. Treating digital security as siloed or abstract ignores its real-world impact. To build safer futures, stewardship must be holistic, integrating technology, ethics, law, and culture into a shared project of resilience.

Ultimately, the safer digital future is not a destination but a direction, a continual process of adaptation, vigilance, and responsibility. The shadows in the cloud will never fully disappear, but they need not dominate. Through rethinking security, harnessing innovation responsibly, and embracing collective stewardship, humanity can shape a digital world that empowers rather than enslaves, connects rather than divides, and protects rather than exploits. The future is uncertain, but uncertainty is not paralysis. It is a possibility. What matters is whether societies choose to step into that possibility with foresight, courage, and commitment.

The journey through the hidden layers of the internet, from the shadows of the Dark Web to the machineries of global surveillance, has revealed both peril and potential. The digital age is neither utopia nor dystopia, it is a mirror of human intent, magnified by technology. Shadows will always exist, for where there is light, there will be obscurity. But shadows need not define the whole.

Toward a safer digital future is not merely a technical goal; it is a moral imperative. It requires rejecting complacency, resisting exploitation, and reimagining the values embedded in technology. It demands humility, the recognition that no system is infallible, and determination, the resolve to build anyway, to improve continuously, and to adapt tirelessly. It calls for courage to confront not only hackers and criminals but also the temptations of power, profit, and control.

The safer digital future will not be handed down by governments or corporations; it will be co-created by all who inhabit the digital world. Every encrypted message, every line of ethical code, every push for transparency, and every act of resistance contributes to this future. The cloud may harbor shadows, but within those shadows lie opportunities for renewal. The task is to bring light not to banish darkness entirely, but to ensure that it does not overwhelm.

In the end, the future of the digital world is the future of humanity itself. Technology is no longer separate from life; it is its fabric. To secure that fabric is to secure our collective destiny. And so, the journey does not end here it continues with each choice, each innovation, each act of stewardship. A safer digital future is possible, but only if we choose it.